W9-DFR-959

A Rereading of the Renewed Liturgy

Adrien Nocent, O.S.B.

Mary M. Misrahi
Translator

A Liturgical Press Book

THE LITURGICAL PRESS
Collegeville, Minnesota

264.02 —check. ?
NO R

A Note to the Reader

In the interest of smoother reading of the text for the nonspecialist, two sets of notes are provided:

1. A simple superscript numeral refers the reader to a note at the bottom of the page. In most cases these notes provide an explanation of a technical word.

2. A number followed by an asterisk refers the reader to a note at the end of a chapter, where we have relegated scholarly material for the use of the specialist which would be cumbersome and awkward within the text for the nonspecialist. These notes are by no means necessary for full comprehension.

This book is being published in French by Beauchesne.

Cover design by Greg Becker

© 1994 by The Order of St. Benedict, Inc., Collegeville, Minnesota. All rights reserved. No part of this book may be reproduced in any form or by any means, electronic or mechanical, including photocopying, recording, taping, or any retrieval system, without the written permission of The Liturgical Press, Collegeville, Minnesota 56321. Printed in the United States of America.

1   2   3   4   5   6   7   8   9

Library of Congress Cataloging-in-Publication Data

Nocent, Adrien.
    [Relecture de renouveau liturgique. English]
    A rereading of the renewed liturgy / Adrien Nocent ; translated by Mary M. Misrahi.
        p.   cm.
    Includes bibliographical references.
    ISBN 0-8146-2299-2
    1. Catholic Church—Liturgy.   I. Title.
BX1970.N6213   1994
264'.02—dc20   94-7253
                                                                        CIP

Contents

Introduction

On December 4, 1963, in the Basilica of St. Peter, Pope Paul VI promulgated with all solemnity the Constitution on the Sacred Liturgy *Sacrosanctum Concilium*. This event is considered by some to be at the root of all the blunders and disorders that the Roman Catholic Church has known since that day, in every domain. This book will not undertake a rebuttal of their opinion. As far as we are concerned, this event which we welcome with gratitude represents an enriching spiritual invitation to all Catholics. There is no doubt but that its recommendations may have been implemented a bit awkwardly—too hastily, perhaps, without sufficient preparation of the faithful who have not always understood the changes in the familiar prayers and gestures that they have known since childhood.

It is not the purpose of this book to draw up a balance sheet, for or against the Constitution on the Sacred Liturgy; it is not a work of criticism. Rather, we hope to answer a real need, after the twenty-five years since its promulgation and its practical application, to assess what has been accomplished, as well as what may still need to be done.

Deciding upon a suitable title for the book once it was finished was no simple matter. It was somewhat tempting to call it "The Reforming of the Liturgical Reform," which has a certain journalistic shock-value. But it distorted badly the author's purpose. This volume is not intended as a criticism of renewal, but as a new look at it. Twenty-five years have passed since the principles of the Constitution were first put into actual practice, and with all due respect for, on the one hand, the bases upon which they were made, and on the other, for the appreciable amount of work that has already been done on the liturgy, it may be useful to indicate certain lacunae that are already pointing up some need for further adaptation.

Twenty-five years ago certain changes often could not even be proposed that can be today. Moreover, what seemed at the time to be real progress was the fruit of intense and often theoretical deliberation, and had not yet had the benefit of practical application, a fact which has created some problems for us today. This in no way should be seen as a denial of the very high quality of work that had been done. If a re-reading of the liturgical renewal is judged to be of some use today, it is not because it was badly done, but simply because it was done at a specific time and under specific circumstances which have since undergone some change.

A few concrete examples may be helpful at this point, which will, of course, be studied in greater depth within the body of the present book.

Every scholar of the Consilium without exception who collaborated on the Constitution on the Sacred Liturgy knew that the kiss of peace was given, in our Roman liturgy as in all the other liturgies, before the preparation of the gifts, and not just before Holy Communion, as it is today. Each and every one was aware of the history of this gesture. And yet it would seem that not one thought to restore it to the place it had occupied in antiquity, or even to make it optional as to whether it would take place before the offering of the gifts, or before Communion.

In point of fact, no one had much experience of the kiss of peace at that time, for it was rarely given among the faithful but was mostly the privilege of the ministering clergy, who moreover usually observed it in a highly formalized gesture. But now that the whole assembly of the faithful is invited to exchange a sign of peace, little by little a new awareness has arisen of the meaning of the gesture in terms of responsibility and personal commitment, and of its relationship with the commandment of love given us by the Lord. Other more recent developments too have induced reflection on the meaning of the kiss of peace and on its place in the liturgy, namely, the emergence of small groups actively seeking a deeper Christian life in prayer and in good works, and also the reinstitution of a formal catechumenate which has clarified the understanding that the catechumen, although loved of God, may not participate in the Eucharistic banquet. Some of the groups have been granted permission to give each other the sign of peace before the Offertory.

Every scholar without exception was aware of the history of the elevation at the moment of consecration. It was introduced in Paris and the surrounding area to impress upon the faithful the immediate efficacy of the words of consecration. This apologetic practice answered to the needs of a particular locale and was unknown elsewhere, either in other countries or even in the Missal of the Roman Curia in 1474. Now, this introduction has clearly detracted from the greater importance of the elevation at the moment of the doxology at the end of the Eucharistic Prayer. Yet it is no small task to eliminate a practice that has been universal since the missal of 1570. Such a reversal might have been seen as a sort of provocation. It is true that it could have been made a part of catechetics, or made optional, once the greater importance of the elevation at the doxology had been thoroughly understood. Still, prudence dictated not changing the practice at this time, and it has been allowed to remain as such.

The lectionary of the missal of 1570 was rather slim. For example, for the season of Advent there were only the same four readings for the four Sundays, repeated each year. During the week those same texts from Sunday were read again each day. Many other examples of this poverty of text could be adduced, a situation which the Constitution on the Sacred Liturgy has tried to remedy. But this was done in such record time that, with the passage of time, this or that elimination came to be regretted, a textual sequence or lack of cohesion was decried. By now the Church has lived six times through the three cycles of proposed readings. It was inevitable that some of the deletions would be missed, or that the juxtaposition of two cycles of continuous readings would attract some criticism—such as the second readings and the Gospels of the Sundays in Ordinary Time. These shortcomings were not sensed while the lectionary was being worked on, but they became obvious after concrete experience.

When the numbers of biblical texts are increased, supporting teaching must accompany them, or the additions will bear no fruit. Would it be feasible to provide a place for this teaching during the week, by, say, simplifying certain rites or chants which, moreover, had been only gradually introduced into the Liturgy of the Word?

We hope that these examples are sufficient to illustrate the point that it may not be possible to accomplish so much so quickly, at one given point in time, and under all circumstances; and that a constructive reappraisal need not be seen as legitimizing any accusations of incompetence or narrow-sightedness. We would hope that by now the reader understands clearly that this book is intended to be as free as possible of all pretentions, all spirit of negative criticism, and all desire for inappropriate innovation. Besides the desire to explicate in some instances the reasons for some of the modifications in the liturgy, as well as the proposed changes—based on historical fact or on the lessons that experience over time has provided—the author wishes also to make clear that the liturgy is not monolithic, but alive, and like all living things it must always remain open to the possibility of change.

In the interests of smooth reading and accessibility for readers from varied backgrounds and even cultures, the style of the text has been deliberately kept as simple and close to ordinary speech as possible. A double system of notes has been provided: The nonspecialist will find explanations of theological and liturgical terms at the bottom of the page, while the specialist is referred to notes at the end of each chapter that will enable him or her to verify the sources of an established or a proposed practice.

Lastly, we would remind the reader that while it is unquestionably permissible to suggest corrections and certain innovations, it is nonetheless true that no one may actually put such into practice in an official liturgical celebration so long as the competent authority has not yet made any relevant decision. The celebration of the liturgy remains as the Church teaches, and it is not the property of any individual no matter how well-intentioned, even if it could be proven that his or her initiatives are excellent in themselves, and that they would further the fruitful participation of the faithful in the liturgy.

1 The Celebration of the Eucharist

1. The Liturgy of the Word

A. Structure

The commissions which were studying the Liturgy of the Word focused their attention on its authenticity, which had blurred somewhat over the centuries, with a view to re-establishing it. The distortions which this celebration had been subject to over time are well known. Diverse elements were introduced into the simple structure which St. Justin presents in his first *Apology,* chapter 67, and which he described to the emperor Antonine the Pious in 150.[1]* This basic structure had been inherited from the Saturday morning liturgy of the synagogue: Reading from the Law, chants, reading from the Prophets, targum,[1] prayer for the community.[2]* St. Luke tells us that Jesus arrived at the synagogue at the moment when the second and final reading was about to begin. The acolyte handed the scroll to him, he read out loud a brief passage from the prophet Isaiah, and then he returned the scroll to the acolyte; all eyes were riveted upon him.[2]

This remarkable sobriety was not preserved, for a number of complex reasons. We may note, to begin with, pastoral preoccupation with inducing inner recollection among the faithful during the entrance of the celebrant. The *Gloria,* one of the most

[1] A commentary on Scripture. Normally when Scripture is proclaimed and read there is also an exegetical commentary that clarifies its meaning, or explains its application to spirituality.

[2] The Constitution on the Sacred Liturgy, note 5.

ancient chants of the Latin Church, was sung at the beginning of the celebration on Christmas when a bishop presided,[3]* and this precedent led to the introduction of a chant at the beginning of all celebrations of the Eucharist. Like the *Gloria,* the entrance antiphon appears in the fifth century and fulfills its pastoral role by introducing the celebration which is to follow with the singing of a psalm, most often, in the past, Psalm 150.[4]* In the tenth century a prayer called the *apologia* began to be inserted, arising from the feeling of profound unworthiness on the part of the celebrant.[5]* This prayer was at first quite simple, and was reserved to the clergy. *Roman Ordo I* tells us that the pontiff bows before the altar and recites a prayer of veneration,[6]* and, somewhat later, *Ordo VI* specifies that the pontiff is recalling his sins.[7]* In the tenth century, with the evolution of the discipline of penance, it becomes possible to substitute an offering of the sacrifice of the Mass for a long penance for the forgiveness of sins. This development will bring in its train the introduction of numerous prayers of apology. For the missal that he made universal in 1570, Pope Pius V drew on the missal of 1474, which contains a considerable number of these prayers, particularly at the beginning of Mass.[8]*

In the renewal of the Liturgy of the Word this basic structure was modified very little, except that the act of repentance was somewhat further developed, and the prayer of the faithful which ends this liturgy was reinstituted.

Over the ages Christianity lost its familiarity with the Bible, and Latin was less and less understood. The readings lost most of their impact on the faithful. The celebration of the sacrifice of the Mass began to emphasize the presence of the majesty of God, and gradually created an atmosphere of external solemnization and triumphalism in the liturgy. The Renaissance and Baroque periods saw the development of the Mass as theater and as concert, to such an extent that peripheral elements such as the entrance antiphon, the *Kyrie* and the *Gloria* began to dominate the liturgy, with the result that the Word of God was suppressed and took second place. This situation prevailed until Vatican II, at least to some extent: We should not lose sight of the efforts of Pius X concerning music and chant in the liturgy, and the important documents published thereafter.[9]* However, the problem of the Latin language remained a thorny issue.

It is undoubtedly true that a translation is never completely satisfying. This was already a problem when, as early as the third century, Greek texts began to be translated into Latin. So long as there was no danger to the faith, such imperfections as might arise in the translation could not be allowed to hold back the obvious progress that translation represented. For this reason the Constitution on the Sacred Liturgy lost no time in recommending more ample readings of Scripture during liturgical celebrations. Roman liturgy has never had such a wealth of biblical readings.

Nevertheless, with the exception of the *Gloria* and the *Credo* which are often omitted, the structure of the Liturgy of the Word is the same during the week as it is on Sundays. Might it not be desirable for the Sunday liturgy to be somewhat richer, not only with external ornamentation, but in its very structure and in the variety of some of its elements? It is perhaps a pity that those working on the renewal of the Liturgy of the Word did not think of providing a choice of forms for it to take. Certainly there is ample precedent for such variety in several ancient sources.[10*]

Let us imagine several possible combinations which could easily be justified.

The entrance antiphon could be eliminated on ordinary days, as it is in the Liturgy of the Word on Good Friday. The *Kyrie* could include intentions for prayer on certain days. We know from a letter of St. Gregory to John of Syracuse that this was done in his day on Sunday, but not during the week.[11*] It would also be possible to have the *Kyrie* be the response to the intentions for prayer of the faithful.

But a concern for pastoral effectiveness could also justify the return to a more ancient, simpler structure. In fact, it is clear that the faithful would need more Scripture-based teaching. And we know from the *Apostolic Tradition* attributed to Hippolytus of Rome that there sometimes were proclamations of the Word during the week. The author encourages the Christian to pray upon arising, but enjoins upon him or her a preference for attendance at Church "where the Spirit flourishes."[12*]

Aware of this practice and desirous of more ample teaching, could we not permit the use of a simpler structure of the Liturgy of the Word during the week, with the condition that it be accompanied by a homily of at least ten minutes?

One possible formula is the following, which we know of from a sermon of St. Augustine for Easter Sunday: "I went in, I made my salutations to the people, and I took my seat to listen to the readings."[13]* No *Kyrie,* not even a Collect, a form of prayer not attested until later.[14]* After the greeting, the liturgy began directly with the readings. One could, of course, begin with a prayer after the greeting. A number of examples are given us in the varied structure of the Liturgy of the Word of Good Friday.[15]* If we should wish to provide teaching after the Gospel during the week, a similarly simple structure seems particularly well adapted to our times, when the great majority of the faithful do not have the leisure to prolong their presence in Church. Some thirty minutes as a minimum might be suggested for a celebration of the Eucharist with the faithful present.

Several proposals for variety in the celebrations of the Word are suggested below for study (excepting those ordinary days when a homily or other catechesis is given):

1. Entrance antiphon, prayer, *Kyrie* with intentions, (*Gloria*), readings, Gospel and homily.
2. Entrance antiphon, (*Gloria*), readings, Gospel, homily, intentions with *Kyrie* and prayer.

The place of the act of repentance could be either at the beginning of the celebration, or after the homily or the *Credo,* in more than one way:

1. One intention asks for pardon for sins.
2. The act of repentance follows the intentions in the form of a simple absolution, or by introducing the absolution with a prayer for God's mercy.

B. Ritual

We could also take a look at different ways to lead into the chanting or the proclamation of the Gospel:

1. By taking up the book containing the Gospels from the altar, and showing it to the faithful before going up to the ambo.
2. By going directly to the ambo, as is widespread custom today, but which is also the least meaningful practice.

At all events, it would be best not to prepare the Gospel on the ambo before the celebration.

After the proclamation of the Gospel, the book could be lifted for veneration by the faithful, and the person who has proclaimed the Gospel then kisses the text.

This act of veneration of the Gospel could be solemnized in different ways:

> 1. By having the open book kissed not just by the celebrant, but by all the ministering persons.
> 2. If the faithful are not too numerous, by having them kiss the Gospel either closed or open, if this is a possibility.

We have supplied in the notes the historical sources for all these suggestions.[16]*

It seems desirable to inculcate in the faithful deep respect for Scripture and for the book which contains it, as is done in the Byzantine Rite. This is the reason behind the urgency with which the suggestion has been made that a separate book contain the Gospels—indeed, this is already the case in some places, but it is rare. One should never, under any circumstances, use those pamphlets which are passed out to the faithful to help them follow the celebration.

It may be permitted here to introduce a brief parenthesis. These pamphlets distributed to the congregation should only contain those texts which they need in order to make the proper responses, or sing, and should not include the prayers, readings, the Preface, or the Eucharistic Prayer, which they should hear, and not read. If it seems desirable for the faithful to take home the other texts, such as the readings, a supplement could be given out at the end of the celebration.

Obviously, these suggestions concerning the Liturgy of the Word suppose certain architectural considerations, not only for the new construction of churches, but also for the remodeling of the old.

Based on the Book of Esdras (8 and 9), synagogues are always built with a special place for the proclamation of the Scriptures. Syrian churches had, in the nave, a *bêma,* an ambo for this purpose. In Western liturgy, the ancient churches always had an ambo, but rather than being in the middle of the nave, it was at the side, or at the beginning of the nave. The principal ancient ambos that have been preserved or restored are well-known. During the Renaissance the major significance of the ambo was lost sight of, and they were suppressed, as, for example, in Rome.

C. Contents

It is undeniable that the reworking of the lectionary has been one of the most important and most fundamental tasks of renewal. To restore to Christians frequent and varied exposure to Scripture, especially through the liturgy, means working with the power of the Spirit to influence their way of thinking, their conception of the divine Persons, the Church and her sacraments. It is still too early to make an objective assessment of the results so far. But it would not be premature to assert that certain ways of presenting dogma and the sacraments are now outdated. During the second millennium the catechesis of dogma and of the sacraments was mainly based on the *Lex credendi,* which is to say that the means of teaching were largely limited to conceptual demonstration and the study of the "mechanics" of the sacraments. Whereas the use of a lectionary such as the one we have now largely brings us back to the catechetical methodology of the first millennium, that is, the *Lex orandi,* a dynamic presentation of dogma and of the sacraments which springs from the historical realities of salvation as revealed in Scripture.[17]*

Another important element is the "rediscovery" during Vatican II of the different modalities of the presence of the Lord, as discussed in the Constitution on the Sacred Liturgy (no. 7). Of those enumerated, the Eucharistic presence is considered the "highest." This gives rise to the question of whether the other modalities of presence are only real by analogy, or whether they possess their own reality which can exist in different degrees. There is no definitive theological study on this point. The magisterium has not spoken, but we should not overlook the encyclical *Mysterium fidei* of Pope Paul VI in which he insists strongly on the reality of the permanent presence of the Lord in the Eucharist. The language he uses is very clear, his thinking is unequivocal. When he describes the Eucharistic presence as real, he is not saying that the other modalities are not, but he affirms that in the

Eucharist the presence of the Lord is real "to the highest degree." This does not mean that the presence is not real in the other modalities.[18]* If I baptize, it is the Lord who baptizes, but once the baptism has taken place, the water is just water as it was before, and the presence of the Lord is no longer there. If I proclaim Scripture in the liturgical assembly, once the reading is over, the book is merely a book and that particular modality of the presence of the Lord is no longer operant. But if I celebrate the Eucharist, there is no longer bread and wine present, it is the Body and Blood of the Lord, and this presence endures as long as the Species of bread and wine are still there. This is the meaning of "the highest degree" of presence. The other modalities are real, but not in this way. And such a theology of the Word proclaimed during the liturgical celebration must surely impart to the lectionary, as well as to the way in which particular readings are selected and proclaimed, exceptional power.

It is not our intention here to go into the history of the lectionary. But a few remarks are indispensable if the reasons for what we have to say about the second readings of Sundays in Ordinary Time are to be clearly understood. The discussion will be limited to those particular readings.

It required much deliberation, but finally it was decided to organize these Sundays into three cycles of readings, spread out over three years. The Synoptic Gospels would be read continuously, in order, as much as possible. The Gospel of John would keep its traditional place in Lent and Eastertide. It was also decided to pair together, approximately, the first reading (from the Old Testament) and the passage from the Gospels. This rough pairing was already in place for the different liturgical seasons, as, for instance, in the readings for the Sundays in Eastertide. So this was no innovation, but since the importance was also recognized of giving the faithful a continuous reading from Scripture—which had been done for the Synoptics—the suggestion was made to do the same thing for the Epistles. The group studying the question found the idea attractive, and we see the results in the lectionary.

How well is this system working, now, after twenty-five years? Opinions may differ: Many, in particular biblical scholars, are happy with the continuous reading, both for themselves and for the faithful, who will thus come to know Scripture better. But there are some who look to antiquity, as well as to quite recent times, and are of the opinion that it is a mistake to overdo these pairings, even when done only approximately, and that we should let Scripture speak for itself. With all due respect for this opinion, which has its justifications, we must still not forget that there is an important difference between reading the Bible and drawing exegetical interpretation from it, and proclaiming the Bible as the Church does with another spiritual interpretation, chosen not in contradiction with the first, but from a distinctly other viewpoint. The Church's understanding of a particular text, and especially of the Gospels, is manifest from the choice of preceding readings. A particularly clear example is the First Sunday in Lent, Cycle A. On this day catechumens can give their chosen name in order to receive instruction and the exorcisms preparatory to their baptismal initiation. The liturgy for the day proclaims for their benefit Genesis 2:7-9 and 3:1-7, which relate the creation of the world, and the temptation and fall of Adam and Eve. The choice for the Gospel reading, Matthew 4:1-11, acts as a prism through which to look at the first reading: It tells of the victory of Christ over the temptations offered him by Satan. The second reading, Romans 3:12-19, delves into the deeper meaning of the first and the third readings: Where sin abounds, there is abundant grace. In this instance the liturgy is actually giving an interpetation of these texts by the act of their proclamation. It may be obvious to the exegete that these three readings have no particular affinity, but we see here the intention of the Church, clearly enriching, attaching greater importance to the catechetical value of this sequence of texts than to the importance of providing a continuous reading of Scripture with no particular point of view.

In the case of Sundays in Ordinary Time, the particular meaning of the Gospel is determined by the first reading, but the second one, since it is continuous with that of preceding weeks, bears no relationship. The result is another element of value in itself but which cannot be a part of the first reading and the Gospel, nor even a complement to them, unless it is pulled and squeezed out of shape in order to try and force it into the perspective of the preceding readings, a process likely to do considerable distortion to the text itself. This problem has been obvious to the faithful, who, by now, after twenty-five years, are used to a certain degree of coherence in the readings. So the very opposite of what was wanted happened. In a significant number of parishes the second reading is no longer proclaimed, for pastoral reasons that fall within the rubrics and which justify this omission: It is impossible to use the second reading in the homily with any coherence. It might be objected that the second reading itself might be the subject of the homily, but we do not find such a practice either possible or right. For it is obvious that the Gospel is the high point of the Liturgy of the Word, and to ignore this would be neither legitimate nor good catechetics. We must bow before the facts, and not blame the faithful for having been imbued with the meaning of the Liturgy of the Word which, moreover, we have tried to teach them.

In conclusion, it seems a good idea to suggest, as an appendix, yet another choice, which would not require any change in the lectionary for Sundays in Ordinary Time. A study group has proposed another series of second readings more in harmony with the two others. This proposal is of course offered only as preliminary: It remains to be determined whether this new system totally eliminates some epistles from all the cycles, and whether there might not be some readings repeated too close to each other, etc. Smoothing out these wrinkles will be easy once the principle behind the new selection has been agreed upon.[19*]

The following table offers suggested readings for the Sundays in Ordinary Time for three cycles, beginning with the Gospel and the Old Testament and leading up to the second reading.

On the right are suggestions of themes, which of course are meant to be loosely applied:

Cycle A

2nd Sunday	John 1:29, 34	The Son is sent for
	Isa 49:3, 5-6	the remission of
	1 John 4:4-10, 13-14	sins.
3rd Sunday	Matt 4:12-13	Liberation from
	Isa 8:23–9:3 (Heb)	darkness by the light
	Eph 5:1-2, 8-14	of the good news of
		the kingdom
4th Sunday	Matt 5:1-12	Blessed are the
	Zeph 2:3; 3:12-13	humble and the poor,
	1 Cor 1:26-30	they are the chosen
		of God

5th Sunday	Matt 5:13-16 Isa 58:7-10 Rom 12:9, 17-21	The light of justice in charity
6th Sunday	Matt 5:17-37 1 Sir 15:15-20 Rom 13:8-10	The fulfillment of the Law is love
7th Sunday	Matt 5:38-48 Lev 19:1-2, 17-18 1 Pet 1:14-16, 22-23	Love even of the enemy; the way of perfection
8th Sunday	Matt 6:24-34 Isa 49:14-15 Jas 4:13-15	Trusting in God for tomorrow
9th Sunday	Matt 7:21-27 Deut 11:18, 26-28 Resp. Ps. 1:1-6 Jas 1:19-25	Words and deeds
10th Sunday	Matt 9:9-13 Hos 6:3-6 Rom 12:1-2, 9-13	Sincerity and outward show
11th Sunday	Matt 9:36—10:8 Exod 19:2-6 1 Pet 2:5-10	A holy people, a royal priesthood
12th Sunday	Matt 10:26-33 Jer 20:10-13 1 Pet 3:13-16	Our lives are in the hands of God, our defender
13th Sunday	Matt 10:37-42 2 Kgs 4:8-11, 14-16 2 John 4:6-8	Giving of oneself in love to make manifest the kingdom
14th Sunday	Matt 11:25-30 Zech 9:9-10 Phil 2:3-8	Glorying in humiliation
15th Sunday	Matt 13:1-23 Isa 55:10-11 1 Pet 1:22-25	Receiving the seed of the Word
16th Sunday	Matt 13:24-43 Wis 12:13, 16-19 2 Pet 3:8-9, 14-15a	The merciful patience of God lets the good and the evil grow until harvest

17th Sunday	Matt 13:44-52 1 Kgs: 3:5, 7-12 Jas 3:13-17	Wisdom and the discernment of true values
18th Sunday	Matt 14:13-21 Isa 53:1-3 1 Cor 11:23-26	The multiplication of the loaves in charity
19th Sunday	Matt 14:22-33 1 Kgs 19:9, 11-13 1 John 5:4-5, 10-12	The triumph of faith
20th Sunday	Matt 15:21-28 Isa 56:1, 6-7 Heb 10:19-23; 11:1-2	Universal salvation in faith
21st Sunday	Matt 16:13-20 Isa 22:19-23 Rom 1:26-30	Chosing God who is revealed to the humble and gives them the keys to the kingdom
22nd Sunday	Matt 16:21-27 Jer 20:7-9 Rom 12:1-2	Not to follow the ways of the world, but to renounce oneself and follow Jesus
23rd Sunday	Matt 18:15-20 Ezek 33:7-9 Gal 1-2, 10	The brotherly reproach in charity
24th Sunday	Matt 18:21-35 Sir 27:30-28:7 Col 3:12-15	Forgiving your neighbor in order to be forgiven by the Lord
25th Sunday	Matt 20:1-16 Isa 55:6-9 Rom 11:33-36	Have we given our gifts first to the Lord so as to be worthy to receive his gifts in return?
26th Sunday	Matt 21:28-32 Ezek 18:25-28 Eph 2:11-13, 19-20	Pagans, tax- collectors, and prostitutes in the kingdom opened to repentance

27th Sunday	Matt 21:33-43 Is 5:1-7 Rom 11:1-6	Israel the vineyard of the Lord and his newly-elected workers in the vineyard
28th Sunday	Matt 22:1-14 Isa 25:6-10 1 Cor 10:1-5, 11-12	Conditions for being received into the wedding banquet of the kingdom
29th Sunday	Matt 22:15-21 Isa 45:1, 4-6 Rom 13:1, 5-7	To each his due
30th Sunday	Matt 22:34-40 Exod 22:21-27 (Gk) 1 John 4:15-16, 19-21	To have care for one's neighbor and to love him
31st Sunday	Matt 23:1-12 Mal 1:14–2:2, 8-10 Rom 2:1, 17-23	Forbear judging and do oneself what one makes others do
32nd Sunday	Matt 25:1-11 Wis 6:12-16 Eph 5:8-15	Wisdom keeps watch even during daylight hours
33rd Sunday	Matt 25:14-30 Pr 31:11-13, 19-20, 30-31 1 Cor 4:1-5	Be faithful servants, even in little things

Cycle B

2nd Sunday	John 1:35-42 1 Sam 3:3-10, 19 Rom 1:1-3a, 5-7	The call of God
3rd Sunday	Mark 1:14-20 Jonah 3:1-5, 10 1 Cor 9:12c,16-17	Announcing the Gospel for conversion
4th Sunday	Mark 1:21-28 Deut 18:15-20 2 Pet 1:16-21	The authority of the prophets and of Christ
5th Sunday	Mark 1:29-39 Job 7:1-4, 6-7 2 Cor 12:7-10	Sickness and the healings

6th Sunday	Mark 1:40-45 Lev 13:1-2, 45-46 (Heb) Rom 6:12-14	The leprosy of sin
7th Sunday	Mark 2:1-12 Isa 43:18-19, 21-22, 24-25, Rom 3:21b-26	The Son of Man redeems from sin, wipes out the past
8th Sunday	Mark 2:18-22 Hos 2:16-17, 21-22 (Heb) Eph 5:25b-27	Christ as spouse
9th Sunday	Mark 2:23–3:6 Deut 5:12-15 Col 2:6-8, 16-17	The letter and the spirit
10th Sunday	Mark 3:20-35 Gen 3:9-15 Eph 6:10-17	Victory over Satan
11th Sunday	Mark 4:26-34 Ezek 17:22-24 1 Cor 3:6, 7-9	The humble seed becomes the edifice of God
12th Sunday	Mark 4:35-41 (Gk) Job 38:1, 8-11 Heb 10:22-23; 11:1	Absolute faith in the power of God
13th Sunday	Mark 5:21-43 Wis 1:13-15; 2:23-24 (Gk) 1 Cor 15:20-22a	The person who has found salvation, immortality
14th Sunday	Mark 6:1-6 Ezek 2:2-5 Heb 12:1b-3	A prophet in his or her own country, and among us
15th Sunday	Mark 6:7-13 Amos 7:12-15 2 Tim 1:9-12	The sending of the Apostles on mission
16th Sunday	Mark 6:30-34 Jer 23:1-6 1 Pet 2:21-25	Sheep without a shepherd
17th Sunday	John 6:1-15 1 Kgs 4:42-44 1 Cor 11:21-26	The multiplication of the loaves, foretelling of the Eucharist

18th Sunday	John 6:24-35 Exod 16:2-4, 12-15 1 Cor 10:1b-4	Believing, and being hungry no more
19th Sunday	John 6:41-51 1 Kgs 19:4-8 1 John 5:9b-12	The believer possesses life within
20th Sunday	John 6:51-58 Prov 9:1-6 1 Cor 10:16-17	The body and blood of Christ, true nourishment
21st Sunday	John 6:60-69 Josh 24:1-2, 15-17, 18 2 Cor 6:13-16	Listening to the words of eternal life
22nd Sunday	Mark 7:1-8, 14-15, 21-23 Deut 4:1-2, 6-8 Col 2:20-3:1	Going against human tradition and following the commandments of God

(In this passage from the Gospel, verse 18, which is central to the text, should be proclaimed out loud.)

23rd Sunday	Mark 7:31-37 Isa 35:4-7 Jas 1:19, 22-25	Keeping one's ears open, listening to the Word
24th Sunday	Mark 8:27-35 Isa 50:5-9 Phlm 2:6-11	The Son of Man must suffer
25th Sunday	Mark 9:30-37 (Gk) Wis 2:12, 17-20 1 Pet 2:19-21a	Jesus, the Suffering Servant, bears unjust pains
26th Sunday	Mark 9:38-43, 45, 47-48 (Gk) Num 11:25-29 1 Cor 12:1-3	It is the Lord who bestows the charismatic gifts
27th Sunday	Mark 10:2-16 Gen 2:18-24 Eph 5:21-33	Do not separate what God has united

28th Sunday	Mark 10:17-30 Wis 7:7-11 Phil 3:7-14	Leaving behind everything for the wealth which is Christ
29th Sunday	Mark 10:35-45 Isa 53:2, 3, 10-11 1 Cor 9:19-23	Giving up his life to be everything for everyone
30th Sunday	Mark 10:46-52 Jer 31:7-9 Rom 10:8b-13	It is faith which saves
31st Sunday	Mark 12:28-34 Deut 6:2-6 1 John 4:16, 19-21; 5:1-3	Love of the Lord and love of one's neighbor
32nd Sunday	Mark 12:38-44 1 Kgs 17:10-16 2 Cor 9:6-10	The wealth of the person who gives up all
33rd Sunday	Mark 13:14-32 Dan 12:1-3 2 Thess 5:1-6, 9-10	The time of salvation and the reuniting of the elect

Cycle C

2nd Sunday	John 2:1-12 Isa 62:1-5 2 Cor 4:3-6	Jesus transforms the world and the Gospel shines with his glory
3rd Sunday	Luke 1:1-4; 4:14-21 Neh 8:2-4, 5-6, 8-10 Gal 3:23-29	The Spirit which is upon Christ accomplishes Scripture
4th Sunday	Luke 4:21-30 Jer 1:4-5, 17-19 Rom 10:16-21	The prophets and Jesus spoke not only to Israel but to all; but were they heard?
5th Sunday	Luke 5:1-11 Isa 6:1-2, 3-8 1 Cor 9:16-19, 22-23	God calls those who are to proclaim salvation
6th Sunday	Luke 6:17, 20-26 Jer 17:5-8 1 Cor 3:18-23	Happy is the one who trusts in the Lord

7th Sunday	Luke 6:27-38 1 Sam 26:2-23 Rom 12:14-21	Be merciful
8th Sunday	Luke 6:39-45 Sir 17:24-29 1 John 2:7-11	The Word, source of wisdom and the rule of life
9th Sunday	Luke 7:1-10 1 Kgs 8:41-43 Jas 5:13-16	Healing is offered to all who believe
10th Sunday	Luke 7:11-17 1 Kgs 17:17-24 Eph 2:1, 4-7	The Lord restores life to us
11th Sunday	Luke 7:36–8:3 2 Sam 12:7-10, 13 Rom 5:15, 20-21	Love elicits the forgiveness of sins
12th Sunday	Luke 9:18-24 Zech 12:10-11 Rom 6:3-4, 8-11	To confess Christ and follow him
13th Sunday	Luke 9:51-62 1 Kgs 19:16, 19-21 1 Pet 1:14-19	To walk in the Spirit, called to freedom
14th Sunday	Luke 10:1-12, 17-20 Isa 66:10-14 1 Thess 1:1-8	To be ready for the kingdom when it is proclaimed, and to preach love and peace
15th Sunday	Luke 10:25-37 Deut 30:10-14 Jas 1:21-25	Be a Good Samaritan to obey Christ and put his words into practice
16th Sunday	Luke 10:38-42 Gen 18:1-10 1 Pet 4:9-11	Practice hospitality
17th Sunday	Luke 11:1-13 Gen 18:20-21, 23-32 1 John 5:14-16a	To ask boldy in order to receive
18th Sunday	Luke 12:13-21 Eccl 1:2; 2:21-23 Col 3:1-5, 9-11	The vanity of earthly treasure rather seek those things on high

19th Sunday	Luke 12:32-48 Wis 18:3, 6-9 Eph 6:13-18	To await and hold oneself in readiness in prayer
20th Sunday	Luke 12:49-57 Jer 38:4-6, 8-10 1 Pet 4:12-19	The cross as sign of contradiction; read the signs of the times in order to be saved
21st Sunday	Luke 13:22-30 Isa 66:18-21 1 Pet 2:9-10	To be received at the table of the kingdom and belong to a holy people; live nobly
22nd Sunday	Luke 14:1, 7-14 Sir 3:17-20, 28-29 1 Pet 5:5b-7, 10-11	Clothe oneself with humility, the teaching is directed to the humble
23rd Sunday	Luke 14:25-33 Wis 9:13-18 (Gk) Heb 12:25-27	The old ways are gone; we must build while renouncing all to follow the word
24th Sunday	Luke 15:1-32 Exod 32:7-11, 13-14 1 Tim 1:12-17	The God of the Covenant renounces his anger; Christ brings salvation; heaven rejoices in a repentant sinner
25th Sunday	Luke 16:1-13 Amos 8:4-7 Jas 5:1-6	One cannot serve two masters
26th Sunday	Luke 16:19-31 Amos 6:1, 4-7 Jas 2:5-9	The rich and the poor, their destiny to come
27th Sunday	Luke 17:5-10 Hab 1:2-3; 2:2-4 Gal 3:6-11	To live by faith
28th Sunday	Luke 17:11-19 2 Kgs 5:14-17 Eph 2:5-6, 8-10	Our gratitude, we who are saved by grace
29th Sunday	Luke 18:1-8 Exod 17:8-13 1 Tim 2:1-3, 8	The Lord hears and answers prayer

30th Sunday	Luke 18:9-14 Sir 35:12-14, 16-18 (Gk) 2 Cor 12:7-10	Strength lies in weakness
31st Sunday	Luke 19:1-10 Wis 11:22–12:2 Titus 3:3-7	The Lord saves what is lost
32nd Sunday	Luke 20:27-38 2 Macc 7:1; 22:9-14 1 Cor 15:51, 53-58	The Lord is the God of the living
33rd Sunday	Luke 21:5-19 Mal 3:19-20 2 Thess 2:1-4, 13-17	In patience we shall possess life

The second readings proposed here are only suggestions; a final choice will have to be made in a workshop.

The importance of such reworking of the second readings should not be underestimated, however. It is no secret that a large number of parishes, in France, Germany, Belgium, and other countries, are skipping the second reading because it introduces a theme that does not fit in with the two principal readings. Unless we admit that there is a problem here, we may be encouraging what is in fact an act of disobedience that a number of persons might find legitimate, faced as they are with a categorical refusal and what could be considered a blocking tactic on the part of specialists in Scripture and in the liturgy who have no pastoral concerns at heart. In fact, for all the major liturgical seasons, we have been encouraged to work within fairly broad themes, and pastors who have been taught to do so might find a refusal to work out this particular problem an incomprehensible and stubborn lack of cooperation. It would be possible, of course, to leave the lectionary just as it is, but there is no reason not to suggest a choice of second readings for the Sundays in Ordinary Time.

D. The Euchology

Some countries have composed Collects that correspond to the themes of the readings in all three cycles. Experience has taught that this practice is of considerable pastoral value.

But this very experiment has made us face a painful but unavoidable fact: In very many cases a simple translation from the Latin text is not satisfactory. The genius of Latin conciseness is often impossible to translate into another language, with the result that translated prayers are often somewhat incomprehensible. One can understand the hesitations of some Latinists and others who, quite justifiably, treasure our old traditions.

Let us take, for example, the ritual of Christian initiation for adults. New prayers have been composed, expressing the same ideas as the ancient prayers but more adapted to our language. The problem also arises, on many occasions, for the prayers of the Mass. So the question must be asked, despite some undeniable inner conflict, whether there might not be an advantage to composing new prayers which take up the same theme as the ancient prayers, but treat it in a way that is more in harmony with our modern tongue—in other words, not do an actual translation. Admittedly, the very suggestion evokes fear of losing an ancient treasure; and yet one might legitimately ask whether safekeeping a treasure should take priority over the people's need to meet their God in full and lucid consciousness. As uncomfortable as we may be with this issue, it still seems necessary to at least raise the question.

2 The Liturgy of the Eucharist

A. *The Preparation of the Gifts*

a) *The rite and the prayers*

The Liturgy of the Word normally ends with what we call nowadays "the prayer of the faithful," where specific intentions for prayer are expressed by the community. This prayer has been restored since Vatican II. The earliest sure reference to this prayer dates to 150, in the *First Apology* of St. Justin, written to Antoninus the Pious.[20]* Here he mentions the kiss of peace exchanged among Christians. Precisely when this kiss was given is hard to say for sure, but it seems to have taken place at the end of the prayer of the faithful; in any case, it was exchanged before the beginning of the Liturgy of the Eucharist.

In point of fact, the kiss of peace given before beginning the celebration of the Eucharist has its biblical precedents: Exchanged before Communion, it emphasizes the need for mutual love before receiving the Eucharist.[3] This practice was the one which prevailed in Africa, and it also reached Rome.[21*]

Clearly, both places in the liturgy for the kiss of peace are of value, although the specific emphasis is different. The exchange before beginning the Eucharist underlines the need for reconciliation, but it also emphasizes the need to be of one body through baptism. Given before Communion, it places more emphasis on mutual love. Perhaps there is an advantage to allowing the choice, without undue fear of diversity from group to group. A little flexibility will do no damage to the vitality of Christian assemblies.

Our modern missal avoids the word "offertory" for the beginning of the Eucharistic celebration, and for good reason. The word was not well chosen, and can lead to confusion. The prayer over the bread began with "Accept, O Lord . . .," and called the bread the "spotless host." The prayer over the wine began with "We present to You. . . ." These prayers are those of the missal of 1570 which in turn were taken from the missal of 1474, which took them from "apologies"[4] contained in divers missals from Italy and other countries. They erroneously insisted too much on the offerings, which in fact do not take place at this moment, but rather after the consecration, when the Church offers together with Christ himself his sacrifice after it has taken place. These prayers have now been rightly emended. They had their origin, moreover, in a penitential rite introduced in the tenth century, called the "commutation."[22*]

Instead of making lengthy satisfaction for sins committed, one had the choice of having Masses celebrated. This is the origin of those new insertions, usually recited by the celebrant, asking for pardon for sins. One reading of the prayers of preparation over the gifts in the missal of Pius V is enough to convince one of the need to change the prayers of this part of the Mass. Another restitution has been made: Namely, the prayer over the water, at the moment when it is poured into the chalice. This prayer had

---

[3] Matthew 5:23; 1 Corinthians 10:17; 12:12-30.

[4] Apologies. These are prayers which ask for the forgiveness of sins. In the tenth century many of these prayers were created and inserted into the celebration of the Mass which sinners could have said to replace an onerous penance which they wished to avoid.

been composed by by St. Leo the Great for Christmas[23]* and had been interpolated. It has now been restored and put back in its place, as the Collect for the Mass of Christmas Day.

A last remark on these prayers (and others as well): What is the rationale for saying them softly, in a low tone? At the beginning of liturgical reform it had been decided that obligatory prayers would be recited out loud or else would be used to inspire the thoughts of the celebrant without him having to actually use the prescribed words of the prayer. This distinction has not in reality been observed, and it is not clear which prayers are to be recited out loud, and which in a low tone of voice. For example, the prayers for the preparation of the gifts are said in a low tone if it is a sung Mass. Is this a sufficent reason to separate the celebrant from the faithful? It is the same with the prayers before Communion: They are supposed to be said out loud, or else used for the private prayer of the celebrant alone.

While it is true that the participation of the faithful does not mean that they will say prayers reserved for the celebrant, such as the doxology at the end of the Eucharistic prayer, it is nevertheless only normal that the congregation be able to hear the prayer of the celebrant, and participate in it by their silence.

Another question that could be raised is that of the double Eucharist prayer, one over the bread, and one over the wine, with only one word being changed. The ritual might have presented the bread and the wine together, with one prayer mentioning both. It is true that the Jewish ritual provides two prayers, and ours imitates this.[24]* But since two or even just one gesture of presentation had been envisaged, without any prayer, in order not to place undue emphasis on the beginning of the Liturgy of the Eucharist, there was certainly no compelling reason to impose two separate gestures, one for the bread and one for the wine, with separate prayers. This might be another place for freedom of choice.

Happily, it is now the custom in many parishes for some of the participants to bring forward the bread, the wine, and the water. But one problem remains: That of the bread.

The breaking of the bread, which indeed is the name for the Eucharistic celebration itself, becomes somewhat of a formalized gesture when the "little" hosts are presented before the Eucharistic celebration: "We, who are many, are a single body" (Rom 12:6).

Jewish Prayer (1)	Prayer of Antioch	Prayer of Alexandria	Vatican II
1—Acclamation (2)	1—Acclamation (2)	1—Acclamation (2)	1—Acclamation (2)
2—Anamnesis (3) of the Old Testament	2—Anamnesis of the Old Testament (3) and New Testament (4)	7—*Intercessions* 6—*(Epiclesis)* (7)	2—Anamnesis of the Old Testament (3) and New Testament (4) 6—*Epiclesis* for the consecration (7)
	3—Institution of the Eucharist (Consecration)	3—Institution . . .	3—Institution . . .
	4—Anamnesis of the Mysteries of Christ	4—Anamnesis . . .	4—Anamnesis . . .
	5—Offering of the sacrifice 6—Epiclesis (5)	5—Offering of the sacrifice 6—*Epiclesis* (8)	5—Offering of the sacrifice 6—*Epiclesis* of Communion (8)
7—Intercessions 8—Doxology (6)	7—Intercessions 8—Doxology (6)	7—*Intercessions* 8—Doxology (6)	7—Intercessions 8—Doxology (6)

(1) The basic core of the Jewish prayer of blessing.

(2) Blessed are you, Lord God of Israel—In the Eucharist: It is truly right to praise you. . . .

(3) Recalling and thereby reenacting before the eyes of the Lord what he has done: in particular, the liberation from bondage in Egypt. In the Eucharist, the principal stages of the history of salvation (Prayer IV), sometimes with a single word.

(4) The coming of Christ.

(5) The intervention of the Spirit for the transformation of the bread and the wine, which will transform those who receive Communion.

(6) To you be glory for all ages; In the Eucharist: For him, with him, in him, all honor. . . .

(7) Sometimes a simple prayer for consecration as in our *Roman Canon I*, sometimes a prayer for the intervention of the Holy Spirit for consecration.

(8) Intervention of the Spirit among those who receive Communion.

This act which reproduces that of Christ at the Last Supper takes place almost unnoticed. The Italian missal recommends breaking up at least a few large hosts in order to give more meaning to the act. Clearly something needs to be done to make the altar bread more similar to real bread, and there are groups who are aware of this problem. The very existence of this problem is in keeping with a certain Western mentality that is always tempted to find the most practical way of doing something, at the expense of the value and the "feel" of the symbol. There is much work to do in this area, and we will have occasion to refer to this problem more than once below.

There is still the matter of the *lavabo*. Many find this gesture superfluous, since the act of repentance has been restored to its former importance. But it is not so simple a matter. The origin of the ritual lies in the Jewish Passover rite, at the moment when the father of the assembled family is about to take up and divide the bread. It is an act of purification for him as well as for the guests, who also wash their hands. The gesture is surely not simply utilitarian: One washes one's hands because they are dirty. This might in fact be the case if the *lavabo* took place after the priest has incensed the altar, when he might have soiled his hands. So long as the act of washing one's hands is not overemphasized, or distorted as in Amalarius of Metz's[5] interpretation of the gesture as derived from Pilate's washing of his hands,[25*] it is perhaps not a good idea to get rid of this symbolic gesture that is so clear and easy to understand. Our modern missal reflects no perceived obligation to suppress it. On the one hand, a sort of generalized rationalism might lead us to abandon it, but, on the other, it is only logical to keep it if one wishes, justifiably, to see the Mass not as a representation of Calvary, but rather of the Last Supper.

---

[5] Amalarius of Metz sought signs of the Passion of Christ in the celebration of the Mass, instead of looking to the Last Supper, which the Mass reenacts, and in which the unique sacrifice on the Cross is actualized. His well-known commentaries push the symbolism a little far: For instance, in the gesture of the priest's washing of his hands, Amalarius saw Pilate's washing of his hands when he interrogated Jesus.

b) Theology

Attempting to avoid confusion around the word "offertory" should not lead us to reduce this part of the ritual to a simple act of preparation. Great prudence is indicated here in the interpretation of the historical and descriptive texts. From the time of the *Apology* of St. Justin in 150, where there is mention of the gifts being brought up to the one who is presiding for him to give thanks,[26]* until the appearance in the Sacramentaries[6] (at a date as yet uncertain), the "prayer over the gifts" remained the only prayer until the eighth century; but this in no way means that the act of bringing forward the gifts had no theological or spiritual significance, and was a sort of vacuum. St. Augustine took pains to point out that the faithful who are to bring up the gifts are not just supplying the sacrificial materials.[27]* The act itself of bringing the gifts is expressive of its meaning, whether it takes place before Mass[28]* or during the celebration, whether the faithful bring them to the altar[29]* or the celebrant goes down to receive them from their hands.[30]*

The fact that this obligatory act was reserved to the baptized and the communicants[31]* alone makes it clear that it bears the meaning of the exercise of the priesthood of the faithful in the sacrifice which is about to be offered. It also underscores the link between the presentation of the gifts, the Eucharistic prayer, and Communion. Everyone is to bring their gift, including the celebrant.[32]* It would be an error to see in this presentation of the gifts the entirety of the participation of the faithful, while the priest alone offers the sacrifice. The prayer *Memento of the living* of the first Eucharistic prayer of today (the former *Roman Canon*) prays for the faithful present who offer, or those who offer for them. Towards the end of the ninth century, above all, certain elements from the *Apologies* which we have already mentioned, the *Super oblata* or the *Secreta*,[33]* came to be introduced, and preceded this prayer over the gifts. In fact, one could summarize the spiritual impact of the preparation of the gifts by say-

---

[6] A sacramentary is an ancient liturgical book which contains only those prayers which are reserved to the celebrant for the celebration of Mass, or of the sacraments. Another book, the lectionary, contained the readings, and the antiphonary contained the chants. The *Ordo,* which later became the Ceremonial, gave the order of service of the celebration.

ing that in bringing them we are preparing ourselves to offer and be offered with Christ when his sacrifice will be consummated upon the altar.

B. The Great Eucharistic Prayer

No one would argue with the statement that the single boldest reform of the liturgy was the introduction of several new Eucharistic prayers. The germ of the *Roman Canon,* our first Eucharistic prayer today, is found in the *Treatise on the Sacraments* of St. Ambrose of Milan.[34]* Until today, Roman liturgy has known no other Eucharistic prayer but this one, which was doubtlessly reworded, and couched in very dignified and beautiful language, in the time of St. Gregory the Great.

What were the determining reasons for such changes, that were promoted even by Pope Paul VI? Certainly they are complex; some that might be suggested are authentic, others may be hypothetical. One fact is undeniable: The group which was studying the Eucharist was aware of the absence of any explicit epiclesis[7] in our *Roman Canon.* Pope Paul VI himself was impressed by this absence, and he was in favor of the introduction of an epiclesis, which would have undoubted catechical value for the faithful and promote their understanding of the work of the Holy Spirit, particularly in the Eucharist. At the start, there was no intention of creating new Eucharistic prayers; rather, the group aimed at the introduction of an epiclesis into the Eucharistic prayer as it stood. Various projects were studied. The Eucharist was celebrated before the Pope and scholars with two epicleses inserted into the *Roman Canon,* one before the consecration and one after.[35]* But there was yet another reason behind the corrections. Our sole Eucharistic prayer was not easy to interpret. On the surface, it seemed made up of a number of separate short prayers, and this effect was further heightened by the presence of the same ending after each apparent section: "Per Christum Dominum nostrum." Moreover, this prayer had a complicated structure which

[7] The epiclesis will be studied later, on p. 30. It is a prayer addressed to the Father, asking him to send the Holy Spirit. It usually, but not exclusively, refers to the prayer in the Eucharistic celebration asking for the intervention of the Holy Spirit for the consecration of the bread and wine.

was not easy to follow: It contained intercessions[8] both before and after the consecration.

More easily interpreted were the Eastern anaphores,[9] such as those of Antioch and others of the same type, which kept all the intercessions after the consecration, with the result that the prayer was much more fluid. Therefore our *Roman Canon* was modified to more closely resemble these, and all the intercessions were relegated to a place after the consecration. At the same time those multiple endings, "Per Christum Dominum nostrum," were eliminated. And there were further changes: Our *Roman Canon,* true to its origins, recited the names of the Roman martyrs, those pillars of the earliest years of the Church in Rome. There is nothing the matter with that, of course, except that, apart from the Apostles whose importance is universal, a good number of the other saints and martyrs mentioned here are of less interest to communities in other countries, whose own saints and martyrs, in fact, are given no mention. We know that in the past the different Churches introduced into the Eucharistic prayer the names of local saints and martyrs, which indeed has often enabled us to identify these manuscripts. So the possibility was raised of allowing those names, other than those of the Apostles, to be suppressed *ad libitum.*

As already mentioned, a Mass was celebrated before the pope and scholars, and the conclusion was clear: It is not acceptable to degrade what is an ancient literary treasure, especially when little tangible benefit would be derived from so doing. At this point the idea was put forth of reintroducing some of the oriental anaphores into our liturgy, or else of composing new Eucharistic prayers with some of their desirable features. Another motive behind these suggestions was, to be sure, the desire for a certain amount of variety in the celebration of the Eucharist. Yet another reason was the opportunity that would be thus offered to set forth as an example for the private prayer of the faithful the same struc-

---

[8] Intercessions are specific requests made to God. In the Mass they are found in the Eucharistic Prayer, before and after the consecration, or just after the consecration. It is usual to pray for the Church, the pope, the bishop, etc.

[9] "Anaphore" means "offering." The word is Greek in origin and is used in the Eastern liturgies to denote the Eucharistic Prayer.

ture of prayer as in the Eucharistic prayer. The great advantage here would be that they could then go back and forth between private and communal prayer smoothly and easily, for both would have a similar structure and style.[10]

a) A brief description of these prayers

Our missal supplies us with two kinds of Eucharistic prayer. Close examination of the various known anaphores allows us to distinguish two main types, two different structures in the Eucharistic prayer: the style of Antioch and the style of Alexandria. Our missal contains just one prayer in the Alexandrian style, our *Roman Canon*. All the other Eucharistic prayers are of the Antioch school. It may be of some interest to take a closer look at these two types of prayer.

The style of Antioch is drawn from that liturgy and is the closest in structure to the Jewish blessing, recited in particular during the Passover meal. The Alexandrian type repesents that particular liturgy and is closely related to our *Roman Canon*.

What differentiates these two types? The Alexandrian anaphore contains the following structure: (1) Acclamation: "Truly it is right to praise you," etc.; (2) Immediately come the requests for prayer, called "intercessions"; (3) Next a prayer for consecration, which is sometimes a real epiclesis; (4) The consecration; (5) An anamnesis of the mysteries of Christ; (6) The offering of the sacrifice, the central feature of the Eucharistic celebration;

---

[10] There is apparently much benefit to be gained from praying according to the simple and instinctive manner of the Jews: It is easy to go back and forth between liturgical and private prayer, smoothly, for they are both in the same style. The structure of the typical Jewish prayer is very simple: (1) Acclamation of blessing at the sight of a particular event or other marvel: "Blessed are you, Lord. . . ."; (2) Reasons for this blessing: "You who have brought (such and such) about, or permitted (such and such)"; (3) Requests: "May what we bless you for promote our salvation"; (4) A brief hymn: "Glory (be) to you forever, Amen." Let us make up an example: "Blessed are you, O Lord, for this car; you have given humankind such intelligence that we have been able to make such a machine to spare us some of our fatigue, etc. May this invention be a force for good, may it help extend your kingdom, and cause no evil. To you be glory forever." This is exactly the structure of our Eucharistic Prayers, as will be illustrated in the short discussion of those prayers, and can be seen in the table of comparisons.

(7) An epiclesis; (8) Intercessions; (9) The doxology. Analysis shows that this structure contains two groups of intercessions, one before and one after the consecration, and two epicleses, one before and one after. This is the structure of our *Roman Canon,* our first Eucharistic prayer, which, however, contains two prayers similar to an epiclesis but without the request for the intervention of the Holy Spirit.

The anaphore of Antioch is very close in structure to the Jewish prayer of blessing which is the type of prayer used by Christ at the Last Supper. Its structure is more linear: (1) Acclamation; (2) Anamnesis of the Old and New Testaments, long or short form; (3) The coming of Christ and the institution of the Eucharist, the consecration; (4) Anamnesis of the mysteries of Christ (death, resurrection, ascension, return); (5) The offering of the sacrifice, the central part of the Eucharistic celebration; (6) Epiclesis; (7) Intercessions; (8) Doxology.

The Eucharistic prayer of Vatican II adopted this structure but inserted an epiclesis before the consecration which asks for the intervention of the Spirit to transform the bread and the wine. The second epiclesis is found in the same place as in the prayer of Antioch and asks for the intervention of the Spirit upon those who are partaking of the Body and Blood of Christ.

b) Uniformity in the words of consecration

There is an astonishing diversity in the various formulas of consecration in the different Eastern anaphores which were once in use or still are.[36*] The actual words of the institution of the Eucharist differ in the various formulas, which generally reflect the particular character of the prayer as a whole. This fact bears repeating, in order to allay any and all suspicions of there being something like a magical formula present in these words.

However, the new missal has adhered to uniformity in these words, doubtless for practical reasons, and to make it easier for the celebrant to memorize them. But this can give the faithful the impression that there is some magical power in the use of one particular formula rather than another. The celebrant must respect the formula that is imposed upon him, but it is not the formula itself which possesses any particular power, but the Spirit who attributes power to the words.

St. Ambrose of Milan lays particular emphasis on the dynamism of the words of consecration which he calls *sermo operatorius Christi*: The operant words of Christ.[37]* A careless reading of St. Ambrose's treatise could lead one to believe erroneously that he attributes an exclusive power to the words of the institution of the Eucharist. He does, in fact, insist upon the fact that the consecration takes place through the words of Christ. This emphasis seems to support a medieval theology of the form (the words) united with the material (the bread and the wine). One could conclude from this that, in his thinking, the rest of the Eucharistic prayer has almost no importance. But if one reads these words in their context, it will be apparent that St. Ambrose does not isolate them but associates them closely to the prayer as a whole, despite his insistence on the specific words of Christ.[38]* Moreover, in the sphere of the actual practice of the Church, it has aways been forbidden to use only the actual words of the institution of the Eucharist to consecrate the bread and wine.

c) The acclamation after the consecration

In keeping with an old tradition, our Eucharistic prayers do not invite much participation from the faithful in their proclamation, and this is perhaps regrettable. Certain Eastern anaphores, on the other hand, do offer a number of such opportunities. The suggestion had been made to translate some of them into our language and to integrate them into our liturgies, and certainly this would have encouraged some concrete ties with Eastern Catholics of the Byzantine Rite, as well as with the Orthodox. The opposition which this idea ran into and which in fact blocked it will be discussed further down, in its relation to the epiclesis.

Nevertheless, after the consecration an acclamation was introduced which comes as the response to the words of the priest: "mystery of faith." At this point could we interject the idea of the faithful singing an "Amen" after each consecration—might this be permitted, or even encouraged?

A few observations on the subject of this acclamation, "mystery of faith." First, we must not forget that this mystery of faith is not primarily the Eucharist, but the Covenant, which brings the institution of the Eucharist, the reenactment of the unique sacrifice of the Covenant, fulfilled on the Cross. Moreover, the phrase has been taken out of its original context in the words of the consecration of the wine: "The chalice of my blood of the new and eternal covenant, mystery of the faith."

Another observation could be made here that might be considered somewhat Cartesian (and indeed, it could be argued that in the Eastern Eucharistic liturgies many invocations are addressed to Christ): Roman liturgy typically addresses invocations to the Father, through Christ, in the Spirit. Roman liturgy in its "pure" state does not pray to either Christ or the Spirit, but always to the Father through Christ, and with him, in the Spirit. The two prayers that we still have today in the Mass before Communion that are addressed to Christ are not of Roman origin. The entire Eucharistic prayer therefore is addressed to the Father through Christ and his Church. Now, after the consecration we do invoke Christ, with whom we pray to the Father in the Spirit. We are no longer praying *with* Christ, in order to pray *to* Christ: "We proclaim your death, Lord Jesus." Might not we sing instead: "We proclaim, Father, the death of your Son," in keeping with the particular theme of the entire Eucharistic prayer?

d) The epiclesis

The problem facing us here is complex, and opinions vary as to the solution, according to the differing theological schools of thought.

First, an explanation of the term. *Epiclesis* is a Greek word made up of the preposition *epi,* above, and the verb *kalein,* to call. It is a prayer to the Father asking that he send the Holy Spirit upon (whatever intention). Every sacrament contains an epiclesis implicit or expressed. So do several sacramentals, such as the blessing of the baptismal water. In particular, the epiclesis designates a prayer to the Father to send the Spirit upon the gifts offered for the Eucharist. The *Apostolic Tradition,* attributed to Hippolytus of Rome, dating to about 215, contains an epiclesis whose meaning is subject to debate.

The text has: "Send your Spirit upon the gifts, so that those who are participating in the sacrifice be strengthened in their faith."[39]* Some see in this text a prayer for the transformation of the bread and wine, but others do not. In the fourth century the *Apostolic Constitutions,* which take up and develop to a considerable degree the *Apostolic Tradition,* are clearly using the text of the epiclesis in this book, but they add a prayer for the transformation of the bread and the wine: "Send your Spirit to transform this bread and this wine, so that those who are participating. . . ." Since then, Eastern anaphores contain this type of epiclesis after the consecration.

This poses a problem for a great number of Western theologians. How indeed can one ask for the transformation of the bread and wine after the words of the institution of the Eucharist have already been spoken? In this case, it leads one to think that the words of the consecration are not efficacious and dynamic, which is unacceptable. This was the prevailing position in the group which worked on the Eucharistic prayers. For this reason the suggestion to translate into our languages some of the Eastern anaphores was voted down, by one vote, precisely because they contain an epiclesis after the consecration which prays for the transformation of the bread and wine. This rigid stance seems hard to understand. For there are Catholic priests who celebrate in the Eastern liturgies and use these anaphores with this sort of epiclesis unchanged, and they believe in the efficacy of the words of the Institution.

In the Byzantine Rite, the celebrants present the bread and the wine at the moment when they say, "This is my Body, this is my Blood," making clear that they believe in their transformation. The result was that a group of Western theologians took this hard line and brought about the insertion of two epicleses into the new Eucharistic prayers, one before the consecration, asking for the intervention of the Spirit in the transformation of the bread and wine, and the other after the anamnesis and the offering, asking that those who receive Communion be strengthened in unity. The introduction of this epiclesis before the consecration was based on the structure of the Alexandrian anaphores. These do contain an invocation before the consecration, but usually it is a prayer for consecration, and not always a true epiclesis.

Is this really an important issue, and should it not be left up to the theologians? We think not. In fact, by creating an epiclesis before the consecration, we are asking for the intervention of the Spirit for the transformation of the bread and wine. In the epiclesis which follows consecration, we are asking for the transformation of those who receive Communion. We shall not be arguing for the position that this transformation of those who receive Communion is a result of the transformation of the bread and wine by the Spirit. On the contrary, the Eastern epiclesis, taking the Byzantine as an example, asks for the transformation of the bread and wine so that those who participate be transformed. It would seem better to see in this Eastern epiclesis not so much an insistent prayer for transformation, which was already effected by the words of institution, but as reinforcing the fact that the transformation of the participants depends on the transformation of the gifts, by the Spirit.

On this point our Eucharistic prayers are somewhat deficient. The question arises whether there might not be some way to reconcile the position of our Western theologians with the use of the one epiclesis. We could suppress the first epiclesis now in use, which asks for the consecration, and create another one, which would occupy the same place after the anamnesis and the offering, along these lines: "Father, send your Spirit upon these gifts which have already been transformed into the Body and Blood of your son, so that those who participate in these transformed gifts be transformed also, in unity."

Bringing together these two transformations might have some importance for an understanding of the dynamics of the Spirit, as well as of the fullest meaning of the Eucharist, which should not be seen only as the Real Presence, but also in the light of its ultimate meaning in the building up of the Church.

The meaning of the epiclesis does not seem to have been universally understood. For example, in one series of our Eucharistic prayers, the epiclesis following the consecration goes as follows: "Lord, send us the Spirit of your love." This type of epiclesis has nothing to do with the Eucharist and can be used anywhere, at any time. It seems strange that this particular form was adopted.

e) The doxology

The doxology is a very short hymn which, in fact, returns to the beginning of the Eucharistic prayer and its purpose: To give glory to the Father through Christ in the Spirit. This prayer is an intimate part of the Eucharistic prayer; it is a priestly prayer, and obviously is to be recited by the presiding celebrant. It is an error

of pastoral theology to have the whole assembly recite the doxology: Their part is to chant with all solemnity the Amen.
At the end of our Eucharistic prayers the doxology was made uniform with the one in the *Roman Canon*. This is why our second Eucharistic prayer, which comes from the *Apostolic Tradition*, ends with the doxology from the *Roman Canon*, abandoning the original, very meaningful doxology. This concern with uniformity is doubtless part of our Western mentality with its love for practicality: There is thereby no problem with the singing, and the celebrant knows the doxology by heart and will not make a mistake.

Nevertheless, it does seem as if we have thereby lost the richness of the original doxology, and the possibility of varying it according to the particular Eucharistic prayer used at any one time. Such variety existed in many Eastern anaphores, of which we have examined over forty.[40]* Some anaphores contain a doxology directly related to the epiclesis, which is understood as a prayer of intercession, and others are related to the intercessions. We refer the reader to the article cited in the notes for a detailed discussion of this point; here we will limit ourselves to a few examples.

The *Apostolic Tradition* provides the following anaphore, considerably reworked, however, including its particular doxology which is a continuation of the epiclesis:

> We ask you to send your Holy Spirit upon the offering of the holy Church . . . give to those who participate in it to be filled with the Holy Spirit, for the strengthening of their faith in the truth, so that we may praise and glorify you through your child Jesus Christ through whom (may there be) glory and honor to you with the Holy Spirit in the holy Church now and forever.[41]*

There could scarcely be a better description of the final goal of the work of the Spirit: To transform the gifts, so that those who partake of the transformed gifts be transformed too, in order to be able to give praise and thanks. When we abandoned this doxology in favor of a sole form for all the Eucharistic prayers, we lost both the specific richness of the doxology of the *Apostolic Tradition,* and, at the same time, the opportunity of an excellent catechesis of the Holy Spirit and the Eucharist. This unity between the doxology and the epiclesis is of particular interest for

Eucharistic theology. What we have here is an essential and dynamic theology: The Paschal mystery of Christ and its reenactment in the commemoration of the Eucharist lead to the principal goal of being enabled to give glory to God with the Persons of the Trinity, today and for all time. The action of the Spirit consists in unifying the faithful who partake of the gifts, which then enables them to give glory to the Father. Indeed, the deepest meaning of the Eucharist is expressed in the reunification of creation which, although willed by God, was impaired by the Fall. The Eucharist is God's response, the act of love of the Father who wills to reconstruct the unity of creation, for his glory.

This theme of the glorification of God in unity is common to several anaphores:

> . . . so that all who participate in the holy mysteries be united among each other, and filled with the Holy Spirit in order that their faith may be strengthened and that they may always be able to sing the doxology ("ut tribuant tibi semper doxologiam").

This anaphore is the one in the *Testamentum Domini,* a document derived from the *Apostolic Tradition*; both give the doxology as a continuation of the epiclesis and its goal.[42*]

In the anaphore of the Holy Apostolic Fathers (the ancient Eastern anaphore), we read, directly following the epiclesis:

> Gather them together and give to all who are about to receive his Body and Blood to be filled with the Spirit, for their sanctification and the strength of their faith, so that they may proclaim and praise you.[43*]

Other anaphores link the doxology to the intercessions. One example:

> Remember, O Lord, those who bear fruit and do good among the saints of your Church . . . and grant us to glorify you with one mouth and one heart, and to praise your revered and great name, of the Father, the Son, and the Holy Spirit, now and forever.[44*]

Further examples are surely unnecessary to make the point that there could be important advantages to linking the doxologies to the different Eucharistic prayers more than is now the practice.

A further comment on the gesture which accompanies the doxology: As we have seen above in the Introduction, it has proven impossible to eliminate the elevation, even though it was the creation of a local community—Paris—and was a part of the penitential aspect of the liturgy.

This twelfth-century innovation also was intended to emphasize the immediate efficacy of the words of the institution of the Eucharist, so that it be made clear that the bread can be consecrated by itself, without waiting for the wine to be also. This elevation, however, considerably reduced the impact of the elevation of the bread and the wine at the doxology. It is understandable that some would hesitate to suppress the first elevation in order to restore the doxology to its original importance. But if the rite of the doxology were progressively given back all its proper value, it would no longer be so difficult to eliminate the two elevations at the consecration.

We might envisage a very high elevation of the bread and the chalice, a true exhibiting, with both arms raised and kept raised through the response, "Amen." This last point should be stressed. Then after this "Amen," with the celebrant still holding up the bread and the wine, there could be a deep bow of adoration on the part of the faithful, held until the celebrant places the bread and the chalice back on the altar and begins the introduction to the Our Father.

f) Communion

Our discussion will be limited to the prayers of preparation and of thanksgiving. First, however, are a few observations: The *embolismus*[11] of the *Pater* is attested to in a number of ancient witnesses. It is a sort of commentary on the *Pater*. Some of our liturgical books contain diverse forms of this *embolismus*,[44*] which is present in all the liturgies except for the Byzantine. The new missal has introduced, after this *embolismus,* the final doxology of the *Pater* which we find in the *Didache:*[45*] "For to you belong the power and the glory. . . ."

---

[11] *"Embolismus"* means the development of a phrase which expresses a concept or a wish. The *Pater*, which ends with "Deliver us from evil," is followed by an *embolismus* which further develops this request: "Deliver us from every evil, Lord, and give peace to our time."

A number of scholars wanted to suppress the *embolismus* in order to add this doxology to the end of the *Pater*, which is clearly its correct place. But in the end it was the old and universal tradition which prevailed. This does not mean, however, that it is forbidden to reflect upon the choice behind this small reform that was voted down. Either the doxology is introduced, but in that case it should be where it belongs, after the *Pater*. Or, if this is done, perhaps the *embolismus* which follows as a commentary on the last request of the *Pater* should not be left in, and we must resign ourselves to suppressing it?

The kiss of peace has already been discussed in the Introduction apropos of the bringing of the gifts, and will not be gone into further.[12]

The breaking of the bread and Communion: We have already said a few words above on the bread used for the Eucharist. Here we would like to emphasize an issue that is rarely perceived by that practical mentality of the West, but which has great importance for the meaning and impact of the Eucharistic celebration. It would seem that the rubrics of the missal should prescribe, and do so with some strictness, using the bread consecrated during the current Mass for Communion, and not hosts consecrated at a previous Mass.

This last should only be permitted in cases of extreme urgency, and only when a Liturgy of the Word is being celebrated outside of Mass. Our Western penchant for what is "valid" and practical can lead us to neglect, with grave consequences, the value of the meaningful act. It is true, of course, that Christ is present in the Eucharist kept in the tabernacle, but it is also clear that this bread kept over from a previous Mass does not present exactly the same meaning as the bread which has just been offered and consecrated for the doxology and the thanksgiving of the congregation. It is not easy to convince a good number of celebrants (and sacristans) of this. For in order to do so, forethought and planning would be necessary: The faithful would have to be directed to place their host in the receptacle at the entrance to the church, which means someone would have to be there to help direct them; whatever hosts are left over in the ciborium would have to be consumed, perhaps by distributing more than one to

---

[12] See p. viii.

each communicant. Extra planning and work of this kind is not welcomed everywhere; it seems it must be. Our practice of distributing presanctified hosts during the celebration of the Eucharist astonishes and scandalizes our brethren of the Eastern Rites.

The commixtion is the act of dropping a small piece of the bread into the chalice at the breaking of the bread. What actually is the significance of this act for us today, and what was its meaning in the past?

This act has in fact a complex history. When the bishop of Rome would go up to the altar to celebrate the Eucharist, an acolyte, standing in the middle of the nave, would present to him a small chest containing the Eucharistic Species left over from the last celebration. At the breaking of the bread, this hard bread (for back then leavened bread was used) was put into the chalice in order to soften it so it could be consumed. This was a first kind of commixtion.[46]* A second kind was the rite of the *fermentum,*[47]* which the priest delegated by the bishop to serve Mass in some other parish of Rome received from him. The priest dropped this piece of consecrated bread into his chalice. Yet a third type of commixtion arose from the situation where the bishop was ill, and had himself replaced. His replacement would drop a piece of his own consecrated bread into the chalice, as a symbol of his being delegated, and of unity with the bishop.[48]* We might have kept this last type of commixtion as the meaning for ours, even though it has lost some of its real significance. It would connote the relationship of the priest with his superior, the bishop.

However, this is not the meaning actually attributed to this act today. It is now accompanied by a prayer in a low tone (why?) giving this gesture a meaning of dubious validity: "May the Body and Blood of Jesus Christ reunited in this cup nourish in us eternal life." This would be meaningful if the Body and Blood, that is, the bread and wine, had first been united to each other and then separated, and then reunited once again in the chalice. We seem to have fallen back, here, into a symbolism that one might have thought we had gone beyond. The meaning of the symbols of the Mass are not to be looked for in the death or resurrection of Christ. The Mass is a reenactment of the Last Supper which was intended to be repeated. Through the act of the Last Supper, which contains no symbols of the Passion, the sacrifice of

Christ is actualized. Attributing to its meaning symbolic of the Passion makes the catechesis of the Mass difficult to frame and to teach. In our opinion, either the commixtion should be dropped, or it should be given the meaning of the relationship to and unity with the bishop when we celebrate the Eucharist.

As to the prayers before the kiss of peace and before Communion, it seems that a principle solidly established at the very start of liturgical reform has been lost sight of. All the prayers prescribed for the celebrant are to be said out loud, or else they are merely suggestions. The prayer which precedes the kiss of peace was said in a low tone in the previous missal, and in our current one it very rightly is directed to be said out loud. Two prayers have been left for the celebrant's preparation for Communion, at his own choice. They are composed in the first-person singular and, as such, ought not to be obligatory, but used as suggestions for the priest's personal preparation. It would perhaps be legitimate to consider using these prayers for the preparation of the faithful as well, and in that case, transposing them into the first-person plural.

Concelebration remains the last point to discuss here. It has been stated, and with some insistence, that concelebration is not a way of solemnizing the Eucharist, but is intended to represent as faithfully as possible the true face of the Church. It is therefore obvious that the most authentic concelebration presumes the presence of the bishop, his deacon or deacons, and the priests who form the presbytery of his diocese. It would be incorrect to think that concelebration as we practice it today represents a return to the origins of Roman liturgy.

Never, in ancient Rome, would two or more priests have concelebrated without the presence of the bishop. There was at that time in Rome a very deep consciousness of what the bishop, in his plenary priesthood, represented. And this to such a degree that the bishop, at the breaking of the bread, would send an acolyte with a piece of it to those priests whom he had delegated to celebrate Mass in far-flung parishes, too far for the faithful to be able to join in the celebration of the Eucharist where the bishop celebrated. When these delegated priests came to the breaking of the bread, they mingled it with the Precious Blood in the chalice, as a sign of unity with the bishop. What we are doing today is, in reality, as far as the Roman liturgy goes, an innovation. We should be grateful for this new creation, however, so long as it does not deteriorate into a way of making the sacristan's job easier, or into a sort of triumphalism where one tries to get together the greatest number of concelebrants possible. It may be that, unfortunately, a normal number has already been surpassed. For the sake of showing unity with a certain tinge of triumphalism, the humbler, but truer, meaning of the Eucharist has been distorted.

Finally, a delicate matter needs to be addressed which, however, has been almost untouchable: The directive in the rubrics that the concelebrants should each pronounce, in a low tone, the words of the liturgy. Most often this directive is ignored. This obligation is based on a rigid theology of the matter and the form of the sacrament, and it concerns the validity of the concelebration. The imposition of the hand or hands is not considered sufficient. However, the concelebration described in the *Apostolic Tradition*[49]* is very clear on this point. The celebrating bishop proclaims the Eucharistic prayer that he has composed according to a particular schema which we also find in this same work, and which specifies that the bishop should not recite as if from memory the text which is offered as a guide only.[50]* This makes it impossible for the others to recite a prayer whose words they cannot know. On the other hand, all imposed their hands during the entire prayer. The superiority and dignity of this gesture cannot be denied. Perhaps one day we may come to see eye to eye on this way of understanding and practicing the rite of concelebration.

C. The Eucharistic Celebration: A Second Look

As we reach the end of this re-reading of the Ordinary of the Mass, it is hard not to be astonished at the nostalgia of some for the Mass ascribed to Pius V. First, this Mass was not a creation of his times. It seems strange that so many people find it natural that an innovation like this be accepted, just because of the name of Pius V, as if the Pope had received some kind of divine revelation establishing this rite. Above all, it is strange that they should think that the sixteenth-century was particularly faithful to the original Last Supper in its liturgy. One does not need to be particularly erudite to see that, on the contrary, sixteenth-century liturgy was even further than ours today from the ritual that Christ actually employed. This is true even in the heart of the celebration, when we use a Eucharistic prayer which closely resembles the form of the blessing used by the Lord.

This nostalgia is indeed astonishing when one realizes that Pius V's missal (which is to say, the missal of 1474, a whole century before the one of 1570 which Pius V imposed as the only legitimate one for those countries and groups which did not have a liturgy more than two hundred years old) merely revived without being able to emend it a type of yet earlier liturgy that contained a number of prayers introduced on their own initiative by priests who were celebrating the Mass for penitents, following the custom which was mentioned above of the commutation for the satisfaction of sins. It is not that the liturgical commission which produced the missal of 1570 should be considered ignorant; it simply did not have access to all the sources that we have, all well edited, at hand today. This commission worked with the means at its disposal, which were very limited, and it worked under great pressure at a time when decisions had to be made with some urgency; at such a serious juncture it was not a matter of top priority if certain imperfections and practices lacking in coherence were allowed to remain.

It is truly hard to understand this nostalgia: Might it be a form of snobbishness, or simple ignorance, or blind conservatism, or denial of the very nature of the liturgy? Whatever may be the causes, this incomprehensible mentality must be awarded the same patient respect as any other psychological state. But this does not mean that some persons, even among recognized authorities, should be allowed to continue causing dissension among the people of God out of a groundless nostalgia, on the pretext that they find what they call "the new liturgy" disconcerting. There have been numerous attempts to restore the Mass of Pius V, out of the motives enumerated above. They continue to divide the Church, whose authority seems to be weak when it comes to these particular troublemakers, although it can at times be harsh and unmoving when other issues are at stake.

Looking over this re-reading of the Liturgy of the Eucharist, we can see how sound the reforms that have been put into practice actually are, concerning both texts and liturgical gestures. In this entire discussion we should really not be talking about a "new" liturgy at all. On the contrary, the general orientation of renewal has always been geared to studying the historical evolution of a rite or text before attempting to change anything. While aspiring to meet the needs of today, renewal has taken inspiration from the most ancient times, going back way before the last missal in order to change nothing without sufficient grounds. The fact that some things could not be done twenty-five or thirty years ago that could perhaps today does not mean that reform was badly done. This has been the perspective from which we have made certain suggestions and proposed some modifications.

Regarding the Liturgy of the Word, two points in particular should be retained:

> 1) The possibility of using a shorter outline, as was done in antiquity. This would hold for liturgies on weekdays, in order to provide catechesis for the faithful, without prolonging the celebration.
>
> 2) The possibility for the second readings for Sundays in the Ordinary of selecting a text which corresponds to the two others. Some suggestions have been made.

All our other suggestions are secondary and have to do with increasing the emphasis on the Gospel and the book which contains it.

Concerning the Liturgy of the Eucharist, this second look at what had been accomplished by reform contains more thought-provoking material. One point in particular concerns the kiss of peace; it was concluded that its place in the liturgy could be left to the choice of the individual, either before the Liturgy of the Eucharist or before Communion. Either corresponds to a particular theological point of view, both valid. A second consideration has to do with the two prayers of preparation of the bread and wine; the question was raised whether one prayer over both the bread and chalice at the same time would not suffice. The criteria for choosing to recite the prayer of the celebrant out loud or quietly were discussed; it seems that, if it is a silent prayer, its text should be seen as inspiration for the personal prayer of the celebrant and not obligatory. If it is, however, obligatory, why not say it out loud? The washing of the hands was also reviewed, and we questioned whether this symbolic rite of purification which was enacted at the beginning of Mass should be repeated here a second time.

The Eucharistic prayer was the object of prolonged discussion, as we considered the various reasons leading to the important innovation of introducing other Eucharistic prayers. This brought us to look at the structure of several different anaphores, and to show how our recently introduced Eucharistic prayers are closer to the blessing used by Christ at the Last Supper. We also saw how much smoother they are in structure, which makes them easier to follow and useful as well in private, personal prayer.

The anomaly of an anamnesis addressed to Christ after the consecration, when we are praying to the Father with the Son, has raised some questions.

It has also seemed to us that uniformity in the prayers of consecration represents a certain poverty of expression and could lead to a somewhat magical interpretation of the words of the sacrament.

Next we described as simply as possible the problem that the epiclesis poses for Western theologians and how the use of Eastern anaphores in our liturgy was voted down by one vote.

We discussed the reasons behind the existence of two epicleses in our Eucharistic prayers and the disadvantage of this situation, which gives a confusing idea of the activity of the Spirit in the Eucharist.

We also tried to show how impoverishing it is to have only one identical doxology at the end of all our Eucharistic prayers, and we concluded that it would be to our advantage to suggest others, appropriate to the particular Eucharistic prayer that they conclude. To give an overall assessment of the renewal of the Liturgy of the Eucharist (we will come back to the Liturgy of the Word), I think that we can praise the work that has been done and still have the courage to recognize its limitations, without being disloyal. To my thinking, what held us back in renewal was the fear—unrecognized—of not staying within a sure, fixed framework, felt as a sort of protection. We were, to some degree, lacking in flexibility, and let ourselves be enslaved to certain overly "divinized" formulas, as we have noted above: The uniformity in the prayers of consecration, identical doxologies, the introduction of almost the same intercessions made at the same place.

All this does not represent tradition: On the contrary, tradition offers a great deal of variety. What we have here is really a sort of hereditary stiffening of the joints, characteristic to a certain degree of Christian Europe. It is as if we needed some sort of secure refuge, and are hoping to find it in uniformity. There is no dearth of examples, as regards the Eucharistic prayers, even other than those cited above. Fortunately, Pope Paul VI did not want the old Roman Eucharistic prayer touched, considering it a treasure that it behooved us to respect. Not so fortunately, however, when it was suggested to use the anaphore of the *Apostolic Tradition*, ascribed to Hippolytus, His Holiness did not show the same respect, even though this particular prayer was two hundred years older than the Roman Eucharistic prayer which he was careful to preserve. In fact, not only was a first epiclesis introduced (and we have discussed the reasons), but a Preface was added, made up of elements of the prayer of Hippolytus itself. The epiclesis which was in place after the consecration was modified, as was the consecration itself, and prayers of intercession were stuck in haphazardly, as well.

We have neglected to point out that there was another addition besides the introduction of a Preface, and that was the insertion of the *Sanctus*, which had had no place in the Eucharistic prayer until then. It would seem, however, that a study of the other Eucharistic prayers shows that, where there is a sung *Sanctus,* in a large number of anaphores there are no intercessions. The epiclesis itself is considered as an intercession, the primary intercession which includes all others possible. And indeed, in this prayer we ask the Father to send the Spirit in order to strengthen in the faith and in unity those who are about to receive Communion, so that they can give glory to God.

Next follows the doxology, which, as we have seen above, is modeled on the very heart of the preceding Eucharistic prayer. It would seem that we wanted to reintroduce an ancient prayer from the beginning of the third century, but we mutilated it out of our need for uniformization. This need was so great that the other newly created Eucharistic prayers were all modeled on the same pattern, as if the series of numerous anaphores which we know of were all composed similarly. Whereas some of these contain no intercessions, while others do; some have a doxology attached to either the intercessions or the epiclesis considered as the major intercession, because, in fact, it actualizes the characteristic qualities of the Christian, who has been given the grace of being able to praise God with Christ in his sacrifice. So there was a lack of flexibility just at the time when work on the Eucharistic prayers was being done.

Not everyone is familiar with the Eucharistic prayer in the *Apostolic Tradition,* or if they are, they may not have made a study of it. To help them reach a better understanding of what we have been saying, we offer below an important table of comparison. It will be seen that the changes which were avoided for the *Roman Canon* were cruelly inflicted on the prayer that was two centuries older. Personally, I cannot understand why we could not accept in our series of Eucharistic prayers the one whose Preface was so close to the heart of the prayer itself. It is all the more surprising that, shortly afterwards, new Eucharistic prayers were composed with a Preface closely tied to the body of the prayer. It is not clear why a Eucharistic prayer could not leave out the *Sanctus,* which is not a necessarily original part of the Eucharistic prayer, nor indispensable to it. Let us say that we drop the epiclesis before the consecration—even though this, as we saw, raises some questions. It is not easy to understand why it was so necessary to introduce the intercessions, and why the doxology had to be changed. Even if these changes were deemed necessary—and it is not clear why—wouldn't it have been better to give up the idea of using this prayer if it had to be so mutilated? Here again we see at work an attitude which is perhaps no longer current, or at least one could hope so.

Table I

Anaphore of Hippolytus	Eucharistic Prayer II
We give you thanks, O God, *through your beloved child Jesus Christ, whom you have sent to us* in these last times as *Savior, redeemer,* and messenger of your will, he who is your inseparable Word, *through whom you have created everything and whom,* ac-	Father most holy, it is truly right and good to give you thanks always and everywhere, through your beloved Son, Jesus Christ: For he is your living Word, *through whom you have created all things; it is he whom you have sent to be our Redeemer and Savior,* God made

cording to your good pleasure, you sent down from heaven *in the womb of a virgin, and who, once he was conceived,* became incarnate and manifested himself as your Son, born of the Holy Spirit and the Virgin.

man, *conceived of the Holy Spirit and born of the virgin Mary.*

Table II

It is he who, *accomplishing your will and winning for you a holy people, stretched out his hands while he suffered* to deliver from suffering those who lay their trust in you. While he gave himself up to voluntary suffering *in order to destroy death* and break asunder the chains of the devil, crush hell under foot, restore the just to the light, establish the rule (of faith) *and show forth the resurrection,* taking the bread, he gave you thanks, and he said: Take, eat, this is my body which is broken for you. In the same way the chalice, saying: This is my blood which is spilled for you. When you do this, do it in memory of me.

In order to accomplish your will to the very end, and gather from the multitude of men a holy people to belong to you, he spread out his hands in the hour of his Passion in order to break the power of death, and to make manifest the resurrection. This is why, with the angels and all the saints, we proclaim your glory, singing in a single voice: Holy! Holy! Holy! . . .

You who are truly holy, you who are the source of all holiness, Lord, we pray you: Sanctify these offerings, pouring out your Spirit upon them; may they become for us the Body and Blood of Jesus, the Christ, our Lord. At the moment when he was handed over and entered of his own free will into his Passion, he took the bread, and gave thanks. . . . *(Here the text of the consecration joins that of the other Prayers.)*

Table III

Remembering therefore his death and resurrection, we offer you this bread and this chalice, giving you thanks that you deemed us worthy

Commemorating here the death and resurrection of your Son, *we offer you, O Lord, the bread* of life and the *cup* of salvation, and *we*

to come before you and *to serve you* as priests.	*give you thanks, for you have chosen us to serve in your presence.*

Table IV

And we ask you to send your Holy Spirit upon the offering of the holy Church. As you gather (them) up, give to all who are taking part in your holy (mysteries) (to take part in them) in order to be filled with the Holy Spirit for the strengthening of (their) faith, in the truth.	We humbly pray you that, having partaken of the Body and Blood of Christ, we may be gathered together into a single body, through the Holy Spirit.

Table V

In order that we praise you and glorify you through your Child Jesus Christ, through whom be glory and honor to you, with the Holy Spirit in the Holy Church, now and forever.	Recall, O Lord, your Church . . . etc. (These are the prayers of intercession for the Pope, etc.)

Through him, with him, and in him . . . . (the usual doxology) |

The resemblances as well as the profound differences are easy to see. We shall begin with some general remarks, and go on to a more detailed discussion.

As we have seen above, it would have been regrettable if an ancient text like the *Roman Canon* had been modified; and surely we should also regret that this even older anaphore has been so mutilated. Why was this done? We see two motives at work here: First, desire for similarity in the wording of the various Eucharistic prayers; and second, fear that certain phrases or prayers may prove to lie outside the orthodoxy of the faith.

Similarity in the Eucharistic prayers: Here we have the reason for the change made in the words of the institution of the Eucharist according to Hippolytus, and his doxology as well, even though it is both beautiful and highly original and rich in theological teaching.

Fear of being outside the orthodoxy of the faith: This is what lay behind the modification of certain phrases and the introduction of an epiclesis before the consecration, as well as the almost total reworking of the text of Hippolytus after the consecration.

Let us take a look at the first point, the similarity among the Eucharistic prayers, considering the problem in a somewhat wider context, and then looking at particular phrases in detail.

The anaphore of Hippolytus is addressed to God, and not explicitly to the Father: "We give you thanks, O God. . . ." However, it almost surely means God the Father, since the instrument of our thanksgiving is "your beloved child."

This expression, "your beloved child," contains a wealth of meaning that we cannot translate. In Greek, the word "child" also means "servant": And here we are reminded of the words of Isaiah and his poem about the Servant who gives his life for the many. Here, when a Preface was being composed, it was the desire for uniformity in style and expression that won out.

There is no *Sanctus* in the anaphore of Hippolytus, and when it was decided to include one in the new text, a phrase introducing it became necessary.

Moreover, it is only good sense to get rid of certain vague expressions whose meaning is not clear, such as "establish the rule (of faith)." But those other very graphic expressions, "break the chains of the devil, crush hell underfoot," which give such a feeling for the period in which they were composed, were perhaps too intimidating, and were left out. . . .

The doxology was undoubtedly altered to fit the chant we use today. But, on the one hand, we could have composed another chant, and, on the other, this anaphore could have been reserved for times when the doxology is not sung, but proclaimed. For it does contain theological meaning that is of considerable interest. Not only does it express particularly well the meaning of the Eucharistic offering, the praise and glorification of the Father, which is impossible without faith and the activity of the Holy Spirit, but it also offers that expression dear to Hippolytus, "with the Holy Spirit, in the holy Church," a phrase that adds a perspective relatively unknown in the West, namely, the decisive work of the Holy Spirit in all that the Church accomplishes.

Now we come to those modifications based on a certain fear of causing confusion as far as theological orthodoxy is concerned.

Hippolytus, in the beginning of his anaphore, expresses in his own way a somewhat startling reality: "Having been conceived, he became flesh, and manifested himself as your son. . . ." A casual reading might lead one to think that Hippolytus means to teach that the Son became the Son through his incarnation, whereas the Son, like the Father, is from all eternity. This, however, is not the thought of Hippolytus. His theology is quite similar to that of St. John, for whom the Sonship of God is above all characterized by the will to obey and serve the Father. He came to carry out the will of the Father, and he can only do this by becoming flesh. This obedience drew from the Father the words, "This is my well-beloved son," at the baptism in the Jordan and at the Transfiguration. He merits the title of "Son" more than ever before by becoming incarnate. He is truly the Son when he becomes flesh. Although he is the Son from all eternity, his incarnation, like his paschal mystery, shows him forth more than ever before as the Son who carries out the saving will of the Father, obeying his eternal intent. Hippolytus says this clearly when he writes: "It is he who, carrying out your will and winning for you a holy people. . . ." This expression, ". . . and winning for you a holy people," which has echoes in the First Letter of Peter 2:9 has somewhat unfortunately been changed into "a people who belong to you," which tends to mask the activity of the Father and his will to seek a chosen people.

But it was the epiclesis that saw the major modifications. We touched on these above, and will make only a few remarks here.

Using two prayers to the Father, asking him to send the Spirit, in a single anaphore is not a new practice. We know that the Alexandrian anaphores contain prayers of this kind. The anaphore of Hippolytus only has one, following the model of the Antioch school.

For the sake of conforming this prayer to the old *Roman Canon,* which contains no epiclesis but offers an invocation before the consecration asking for the gifts to be consecrated, certain scholars wanted to put in an epicletic prayer at this point. The result can be seen in the *Roman Canon* today: "Sanctify fully this offering through the power of your blessing, make it perfect and worthy of you, *that it may become for us the Body and Blood of your beloved Son,* Jesus Christ, our Lord."

The purpose here was to preserve the consecrating power of

the words of the institution. It is, of course, an article of faith that it is the words of Christ themselves which consecrate the bread and wine. This concept of the power of the words is much in evidence in the writings of the Fathers, especially St. Ambrose. His treatise *On the Sacraments* contains the central part of the *Roman Canon,* as we shall see below. He uses a phrase, original to him, to designate the empowering sacramental words: *"Sermo operatorius,"* the eternal, dynamic words.[51]* He uses the exact same terms for the Eucharist as he did for baptism: "By what words does the consecration become actualized, and who speaks them? Our Lord Jesus. It is the words of Christ which effect this sacrament. And what are these words? Those through which everything has been made. He spoke, and it was done; he gave the order, and it was created. Hear, then, how the words of Christ habitually change all creation, and even, if he so wills, the laws of creation."[52]* At this point St. Ambrose gives examples from Scripture.

In another of his treatises, *On the Mysteries,* he continues to stress the dynamic power of the word of Christ: "It is the very words of Christ which effect. . . . For this sacrament which you receive is produced by the words of Christ. . . . The word of Christ, which was able to make something out of nothing, can it not therefore change things into something that they were not before?"[53]*

It was this dynamic power of the words of Christ that were stressed, lest the importance of his words in the consecration should be diminished in importance if the epiclesis which follows the consecration were the only one retained. So it is the epiclesis before the consecration which has as its object the consecration itself, which takes place with the intervention of the Holy Spirit, who gives power once again to the words spoken long ago by Christ and are pronounced now by his minister.

It was not, however, seen as desirable to suppress the epiclesis which follows the consecration in the Eastern anaphores. However, its text was greatly modified.

Hippolytus asks for the coming of the Holy Spirit on the offering of the holy Church. He is not asking for the consecration of the gifts itself, although there are many who read that meaning. However it may be, he has in mind the action of the Spirit in this offering, which consists in assembling the faithful who take part in the mysteries. The Spirit also acts in the faithful to strengthen their faith, in truth. It certainly seems that Hippolytus expresses the meaning of his epiclesis in the clearest possible terms.

The text of Hippolytus has a close relationship between participation in the Eucharist, where the Spirit acts, and gathering together in unity, and the strengthening in the faith. In our Eucharistic Prayer II this relationship is considerably weakened by the splitting up into two distinct places the various elements of the epiclesis of Hippolytus. In the first, before the consecration, we ask God to send the Spirit for the consecration; in the second, after the consecration, we ask that, having partaken of the Body and Blood of Christ, we be gathered together into one body by the action of the Holy Spirit. It is less clear, however, that it is precisely because we partake of the Body and Blood of Christ, through the intervention of the Spirit, that we are gathered together into one body. So the epiclesis has lost some of its force.

Next come the prayers of intercession, which are not found in the anaphore of Hippolytus. As we can see, the Eucharistic Prayer of Hippolytus is of the school of Antioch, whereas the one we use now is a sort of hybrid: It is Alexandrian in that it contains two epicleses, but it follows the model of Antioch by having just one prayer of intercession after the consecration.

It bears repeating here that the anaphore of Hippolytus contains a good number of expressions which are a carbon copy of words typically used by St. Irenaeus, and that we only find in his writings. As such, this venerable prayer is a jewel which we must come to love, to use in our prayer, and to meditate upon. We will have a better understanding of it after we have studied the other Eucharistic Prayers.

This critical overview is not intended to diminish or deny the real merits of the liturgical renewal. What we took pains to say at the beginning cannot be overemphasized: What was done or not done cannot be judged from our present vantage point, but must be seen in the context of the times, and of the mentality of those times.

Notes

¹* Justin, *Première Apologie* (First Apology), Ed. L. Pautigny, 1904, Textes et documents, I, 143.

²* C. Perrot, *La lecture de la Bible dans la synagogue. Les anciennes lectures palestiniennes du Shabbat et des fêtes* (The Reading of the Bible in the Synagogue. The Ancient Palestinian Readings for the Sabbath and Holy Days) Hildesheim, 1973, 15–35; 128–140. Idem, *La lecture de la Bible dans les synagogues,* La Maison Dieu (LMD) 126, 1976, 24–41, with a table of readings.

³* *The Gregorian Sacramentary of Hadrien* indicates that only the bishop intones this hymn, at Christmas (Ed. J. Deshusses [Spicilegium Friburgense, 16] 85, 2). He will keep this privilege until around the end of the eleventh century (*Microloge de Bernold de Constance)* (Micrologia of Bernold of Constance) 2; Migne, *Patrologia Latina* (PL) 149, 979 where we see the priest, not the bishop, also intone the *Gloria.* The *Liber Pontificalis,* Ed. L. Duchesne, or Ed. los Forchelle-Allgh. M. Sticler, *Studia Gratiana,* 1978, vol. 22, 99 (LP 45) attributes to Pope Symmachus (498–514) the extension of the sung *Gloria* to Sundays and feasts of the martyrs.

⁴* *PL* attributes to Pope Celestinus I (422–431) the introduction of the song of entry where Psalm 150 was sung.

⁵* A. Nocent, *Les Apologies dans la célébration eucharistique* (The Apologies in the Eucharistic Celebration), in *Liturgie et rémission des péchés* (The Liturgy and the Forgiveness of Sins), S. Serge lectures, Paris, 1973. Ed. Liturgiche, Rome, 1973, 179–196. A series of Apologies is found in E. Martène, *De antiquis Ecclesiae ritibus, Ordines V, VI, VII, IX, XIII, XIV, XVI.* For more detailed information on these *Ordines,* see: A.-G. Martimort, *La documentation liturgique de Dom Edmond Martène,* Città del Vaticano, 1978 (*Studi e Testi* 279). For Italy, there are numerous *Apologies* which will figure in the Missal of the Roman Curia of 1474 in A. Ebner, *Iter Italicum. Missale Romanum,* Herder Freiburg im B. Photo-offset reprint, Graz 1954, 1–195; 336–338; 373, etc.

⁶* *Ordo Romanus 2, 49 (Or I)* Ed. M. Andrieu, *Les Ordines Romani du haut moyen âge II. Les Textes.* Louvain, Spicilegium Lovaniense, 1960, Vol 1, 83.

⁷* *Or VI, 21,* Ed. Andrieu, Vol. 2, 244 *Venit ad tribunal paenitentiae; Or X 12,* Ed. Andrieu, Vol.2, 353: *Inclinans se pro peccatis suis deprecetur.*

⁸* The missal of Pius V (so-called), after the prayers at the foot of the altar, which are all Apologies (in particular, the *Confiteor*) provides for an Apology for the celebrant when he goes up to the altar: "Aufer a nobis . . . iniquitates nostras"; then when he bows before the altar: "Oramus te . . . ut indulgeris onmia peccata mea." For the offering of the bread: "Suscipe, Sancte Pater . . . pro innumerabilibus peccatis et offensionibus et negligentiis

meis." The prayer of the *Lavabo.* Before saying the *Orate fratres,* another Apology is provided: "Suscipe, Sancta Trinitas . . . et illi pro nobis intercedere dignetur. . . ." And then the prayers before Communion.

⁹* Pius X, *Motu proprio, Tra le sollecitudini,* of Nov. 22, 1903, *Acta Apostolicae Sedis* (A.A.S.) 1909; Pius XI, *Divini Cultus Sanctitatem,* A.A.S. 21, 1929; Pius XII, *Mediator Dei,* A.A.S., 39; *Musicae Sacrae Disciplina,* A.A.S. 48,19; *De Musica Sacra,* A.A.S. 50, 1958, etc.

¹⁰* H. Schmidt, *Hebdomada Sancta,* Herder, 1947, Vol. Alterum, 778–783 presents different structures for the liturgy of Good Friday in the various liturgical sources. This liturgy is undoubtedly the exception, but it does reflect the purposefully archaic structures of the Liturgy of the Word. Five structures are presented, with their sources: (1) Ancient Roman structure—silent prostration, reading, responsory, reading, responsory, Passion, solemn prayers (*Or 16, 17, 23, 24, 30B; -Gregorian of Cambrai, Gr. Ottobonianus, Gr. Reginense, Gr. de St. Eloi);* (2) Gelasian structure—prayer *Deus a quo et Iudas,* reading, responsory, prayer *Deus qui peccatis veteris,* reading, responsory, Passion, solemn prayers (*The Gelasians—Or 30a, 31, 32, 33, Gregorian of Cologne;* (3) A reworking of the Gelasian structure in a single manuscript: The prayer *Deus a quo et Iudas* at the beginning, then the rest follows according to the first structure without any prayer (*Gelasian of St. Gall 800–820*); (4) A simplified version of the Gelasian—prostration, reading, responsory, prayer *Deus a quo et Iudas,* reading, responsory, Passion, solemn prayers (*Or 27, 28, 29, Gregorian of Jumièges, Pontifical Romano-German, Pont. romani of the XIIth century;* (5) One exceptional structure—prostration, prayer *Deus a quo et Iudas,* reading, responsory, prayer *Deus a quo et Iudas,* reading, responsory, Passion, solemn prayers (*Or 32, Pont. of Guillaume Durand, end of thirteenth century*). We have here a restoration of the simple structure of the Liturgy of the Word of antiquity, with a variety in its applications that could be a source of inspiration for us.

¹¹* P. DeClerck, *La prière universelle dans les liturgies anciennes,* Aschendorff, Münster 1977 (LQF 92). This is the the most recent work which discusses this subject as well as the problem of the *kyrie eleison.* It contains valuable sources for the history and the comprehension of this prayer.

¹²* Hippolytus of Rome, *La Tradition Apostolique,* Ed. B. Botte, Aschendorff, Münster, 83, 53.

¹³* Augustine of Hippo, *De civitate Dei,* 22, 8, CCL 48, 826.

¹⁴* It is generally thought that this prayer was introduced in the time of St. Leo the Great (440–461).

¹⁵* See note 10.

¹⁶* J. Jungmann, *Missarum Solemnia,* Paris, Aubier, 3 vols. This work contains many references to different practices, with their sources. For example, see I, 109 for the procession with the Gospel, bowing before and kissing

the book containing the Gospels; 2, 212–226 which gives many details concerning these different practices.

[17]* An interesting study of the theology based on the *Lex orandi* and a theology based on the *Lex credendi* which arose a thousand years later is the book of C. Giraudo, *Eucaristia per la Chiesa, Prospettive teologiche sull'eucaristia a partire della Lex Orandi,* Université Grégorienne, 1989. The author shows how the first gradually changed into the second, bringing about a gradual slippage in theology. See the review by G. Lafont, in the journal *Ecclesia Orans,* 2, 1991, 207–218.

[18]* Paul VI, *Mysterium fidei,* A.A.S. 57, 1965, 764.

[19]* A. Nocent, *Les deuxièmes lectures des dimanches ordinaires, Ecclesia Orans,* 8, 1991, 2, 125–136. The work is that of the students of the Faculté de Liturgie, Saint-Anselm of Rome, in seminar.

[20]* Justin, *Première Apologie,* op. cit., C; 66, 1–3; 67, 4–5.

[21]* For Africa, St. Augustine tells of the custom of exchanging the kiss of peace after the *Pater,* which, before St. Gregory the Great, was recited immediately before Communion: (After the *Pater*) "Pax vobiscum et osculantur se Christiani in osculo sancto. Pacis signum est." Sermon 227, PL 38, 1101; Sources Chrétiennes 116, 240. In the time of Innocent II, in Rome, both practices were current: The kiss of peace before the beginning of the Eucharist, or before Communion. Our modern Roman usage solidified around the end of the fourth century, beginning of the fifth.

[22]* The practice of commuting a penance into a Mass for the satisfaction of sins was introduced towards the tenth century. This is at the root of the practice of introducing numerous prayers for the forgiveness of sins into the Mass. One Mass from northern Germany known as the Mass of Flaccus Illyricus contained thirty-six such prayers. A. Nocent, *Les apologies dans la célébration eucharistique,* in *Liturgie et rémission des péchés,* Ed. Liturgiche, Rome 1975, 179–196. Idem, *L'acte pénitentiel dans le nouvel Ordo Missae,* in *Nouvelle Revue Théologique,* 9, 1969, 956–976.

[23]* *The Sacramentary of Verona,* formerly known as the Leontine, contains nine Masses for Christmas, composed by St. Leo the Great. The Collect of the first Mass is the one which had been wrongfully interpolated and used for the blessing of the water, before pouring it into the chalice. It has now been restored and put in its original place in the Mass for Christmas Day. *Sacramentarium Veronense,* Ed. L. C. Mohlberg, Herder, Rome. Rerum Ecclesiasticarum Documenta, Series Major, Fontes I, 157–163, nn. 1239–1272 (L).

[24]* Several texts from Jewish liturgy can be found in A. Hänggi-I. Pahl, *Prex eucharistica,* Spicilegium Friburgense, 12, Ed. Universitaires, Fribourg, Switzerland. For the bread and the wine, 6, for Shabbat and holy days.

[25]* Amalarius of Metz, *Opera liturgica omnia,* Ed. J. M. Hanssens, Città del Vaticano, 1948–1950, Studi e Testi 138–140. In the *Expositiones Missae,*

I, 225, 238, he gives a series of truly bizarre allegories. He will be opposed by the deacon from Lyons, Florus, in his *Expositio Missae* (*PL* 119, 15ff.) and his *Opuscula adversus Amalarium* (*PL* 119, 71-73).

[26]* Justin, *Première apologie, op. cit.,* c. 67.

[27]* Augustine of Hippo, *Enarrationes in psalmos, Ps. 129, PL* 32, 1701.

[28] *The gifts were brought up before the celebration, in the sacristy (pastafora). This was the practice in Arles in the time of St. Caesarius, who often charges his faithful to bring the bread (while it is still ordinary bread) before the celebration: *Sermons 13, 14, 16, 19, 229; CCL 103, 9, 65, 71, 77, 89, 908.*

[29]* St. Augustine informs us that a psalm was sung when the faithful went to the altar to bring their gifts (*Retractationes* 2,11. *PL* 32, 634; *CSEL* 35, 144).

[30]* *Ordo Romanus I* assumes that the Pope and the deacons come to get the gifts from among the faithful, who do not go up to the altar to present them, as is done in Africa (*Or I* vol. 2, n.6ff.).

[31]* Already in the *Apostolic Traditions,* we note that no one who is not baptized and confirmed may join the group of the baptized and confirmed for prayer (*op.cit.* 55, 21). A synod of Elvira, can. 28. Ed. Vives, Barcelona, 1963, 6, forbids anyone who does not receive Communion from bringing up the gifts.

[32]* *Or I,* nn. 82ff.

[33]* There are various theories concerning the *secreta,* the silent prayer over the gifts: Perhaps it is an imitation of Eastern liturgies, or (more likely, if less edifying) it could have arisen from the celebrant's not waiting for the sung offertory to be finished before beginning the prayer over the gifts in a low tone of voice.

[34]* Ambrose of Milan, *Des sacrements, des Mystères* (On the Sacraments, On the Mysteries), Bk. IV, 14; IV, 21-27. Ed. B. Botte, Sources Chrétiennes 25 bis, 82, 84-86.

[35]* A. Bugnini, *La riforma liturgica,* Ed. Liturgiche, Rome, 440-477, where there is a detailed account of all the discussions of the Eucharistic Prayer of the study groups that met before Vatican II.

[36]* For a better acquaintance with these anaphores see A. Hänggi-I. Pahl, *Prex eucharistica,* Ed. Universitaires, Fribourg, Switzerland, 1968. Spicilegium Friburgense, 12, Anaphores orientales (Eastern Anaphores) 99-415; Anaphores occidentales (Western Anaphores) 419-513.

[37]* Ambrose of Milan, *op. cit.* Bk. IV, 15, Sources Chrétiennes 25bis, 82, 15.

[38]* Idem, *op. cit.* Bk. IV. See C. Rinaudo, *Eucaristia per la Chiesa,* Ed. Gregorian University Press; Morcelliana, 1989, 9-14.

[39]* *La Tradition Apostolique, op. cit.* 4, Ed. B. Botte, 16-17.

[40]* See Hänggi-Pahl, *op. cit.*

⁴¹* See note 39*.

⁴²* Hänggi-Pahl, *op. cit. (PE)*, 219.

⁴³* *PE*, 144.

⁴⁴* *PE*, 229. See A. Nocent, *Les doxologies des prières eucharistiques,* in *Gratias agamus.* Studien zum eucharistischen Hochgebet für Balthasar Fischer. Herder 1992, 343-353.

⁴⁵* J.-P. Audet, *La Didaché, Instructions des Apôtres,* Paris 1958, 170-173.

⁴⁶* *Ordo romanus I, op. cit.* vol. 2, 98, n. 95.

⁴⁷* Idem, 101, n. 105.

⁴⁸* *Ordo romanus II, op. cit.* 109, n. 6.

⁴⁹* *La Tradition Apostolique,* 4, Ed. B. Botte, 10-11, n. 4.

⁵⁰* Ibid. 9, Ed. B. Botte, 29, n. 9. "Let the bishop give thanks as we said above. It is not at all necessary that he pronounce the same words as we have given, as if he were trying to say them by heart, when he gives thanks to God; but let each one pray according to his capacities."

⁵¹* Ambrose of Milan, *Des sacraments,* IV, 15, Sources Chrétiennes 25 bis, 110-111.

⁵²* Ibid. IV, 14, 15, SC 25 bis, 109-111.

⁵³ Idem, *Des Mystères,* 32, SC 25 bis, 186-187.

2 Christian Initiation

1. A Sacrament in Three Sacramental Stages

At the time of the Second Vatican Council the expression "Christian initiation" was scarcely used at all, in favor of baptism, confirmation, or the Eucharist—although this last sacrament was not often spoken of in its initiatory aspect. If initiation was not a topic for study, it was due to the Western practice of separating baptism (above all, the baptism of infants) from confirmation, and especially from the Eucharist, which is usually conferred before confirmation, thus robbing it of its power as the crowning experience of Christian initiation. When the different rituals were published, they did nothing to correct this state of affairs; in fact, they were published one by one, piecemeal, as soon as they were ready for editing.

The first ritual, however, the ritual of the baptism of children, included in its introduction an excellent presentation of the three sacraments of Christian initiation, but this did not carry over into the ritual, which only included baptism. Strangely enough, the presentation of the ritual of adult initiation, which was edited next and contained the three sacraments of initiation (baptism, confirmation, and the Eucharist), omitted the explanation of what "Christian initiation" really is. This surprising oversight was corrected in the second ritual of adult initiation.

We see, then, that Christian initiation is a sacrament comprising three sacramental steps. In the East, the three sacraments of initiation are usually conferred together, even in the case of a very small child. This was true in the past of Roman and Western liturgy too, but for reasons which we will go into later, they were separated. For almost a hundred years now this separation has gone so far as to confer the Eucharist before confirmation, at least in some countries of the West. Such a change in practice requires an explanation, and we shall attempt to give one. This is the reason for beginning our look at Christian initiation with the ritual for adults, which is the only authentic one.

2. A Single Book for Christian Initiation

It will be readily agreed that the publication of a separate book entitled "Christian Initiation" would be desirable. It would contain the rituals for adult initiation, including preparation—that is, the entire ritual for the catechumen, baptism, confirmation, the Eucharist, and the mystagogy.[1]

What is at stake here is not just the question of the convenience from the standpoint of the publisher and the printer of having all the rituals together in one book. There is no question but that only adult initiation can be given the name of "Christian Initiation," since in our day, in the Latin liturgy, children do not receive the three sacraments of initiation one after the other. Still, the ideal could be expressed in such a title, even though it only applies, for now, to adults.

The question might be one of creating a catechesis grounded in history and Scripture which would imbue in the catechumen an understanding of the unity underlying the three sacraments.

Perhaps a synthesized narrative of the history of salvation might be useful, taking as its starting point God's "technique" for bringing about the salvation of the world.

We must start with the creation of the world, seeing in Genesis God's activity in ruling the elements with the Spirit hovering over the waters. We are not speaking here of the Person of the

---

[1] Mystagogy: Instruction, catechesis given to those who have already received the sacrament after having been taught only the necessary minimum. The rest will be taught after the experience of the received sacrament, and this is called the "mystagogy." The greater part of the sacramental teachings of the Fathers of the Church was given after reception of the sacrament.

Holy Spirit, but of its "prefiguring," its "type."[2] This presence of the "Ruah" (breath, wind, spirit) is important, because it unifies all of the different elements of salvation. The poem of Isaiah written in the Golden Age gives an in-depth interpretation of Genesis: The world is created in unity, under the influence of the Spirit. The animal kingdom is created in mutual service, and for the service of man, who lets them give glory to God through him, and by serving him. This reading of Genesis by Isaiah shows us the lamb lying down with the lion, and the little child playing with the snake. These are not just empty poetical images, but concrete expressions of the creative will of God who conceives a unified world. Man himself is created in the image of God. This unitary vision of the world to the glory of God is of great importance.

The Fall, whatever it might have consisted in—we shall leave aside all the hypotheses—succeeded in ruining this unity. From now on all of creation is at war with itself, and humankind itself has lost its true image. But God, because he is God, is love, and he wills to restore the world to a state even superior to that in which it was created. Consequently, from the very moment of the Fall God made the decision to recreate an even better world. To do this, he brings in the intervention of the Spirit. The Old Testament is full of the interventions of the Spirit, in Judges, Kings, and the prophets. Through them God tries to rebuild a Covenant. But his people are so unfaithful that the Covenant has to be renewed again and again.

This last time the intervention of the Spirit will be decisive: The Word becomes flesh in the womb of a virgin. The history of the world is changed. The Spirit calls forth the coming of the Word in the flesh. Just as the Word comes down into our flesh, so do we, in the baptismal font, rise up towards divine life and our adoption. The Word has taken up our flesh, and baptism gives us a share in the life of God as adopted children.

This being-in-the-flesh of the Word must express itself in corresponding acts, for the sake of which the Word took flesh. The

---

[2] A "type" is an historical reality, event, or person which is a point of departure for a future actuality, this time the definitive one, called the "antitype." For example, the manna in the desert is a type which announces the Eucharist, here the antitype. In the celebration of the liturgy, the type and antitype are very important and used constantly.

baptism in the Jordan gives the Word made flesh its destination and its role. The Father manifests him to the world as his Son and, at the same time, his Servant. It is his destiny to announce the Covenant that he is about to actualize. In confirmation, the Spirit gives us our destiny as announcers of this new Covenant. After receiving our new life as adoptive children, we are chosen to fulfill a role in the history of salvation which continues uninterrupted—we are to proclaim reconciliation and the Covenant.

Christ is going to make real what he proclaims by fulfilling his paschal mystery of death and resurrection. By celebrating the Eucharist, which actualizes the paschal mystery of Christ, we fulfill our task and responsibility of collaborating in the Covenant and of proclaiming it in the sacraments: The one who eats the bread and drinks the cup proclaims the death of the Lord until he comes.

It is not difficult to understand and follow the three successive sacraments of initiation. They correspond to definite occurrences in the history of salvation. It is also easy to grasp that the Eucharist is the crowning sacrament of initiation: Baptism gives us our *being* according to God, confirmation gives us our *doing*; to proclaim and actualize in the Eucharist that which is proclaimed. In fact, everything converges in the Eucharist, which lets renewed humankind, directed by the Spirit, be in contact with the actualized sacrifice of Christ and to collaborate in this sacrifice.

A. Christian Initiation for Adults: A return to an *ancient tradition adapted for today*

Going back to an ancient tradition, in particular for the liturgical backdrop to the catechumenate of adults, is only justified because of the inestimable value of this tradition. It was worthwhile to recover this valuable material, without copying the past slavishly, but rather drawing on it and adapting it to the present. It is not our purpose here to reproduce once again this beautiful ritual, one of the finest pieces of work realized by liturgical renewal.

It would be an insult to those who worked on it to state that it is absolutely perfect; any piece of work, analyzed more than twenty-five years afterward, can be expected to yield some points open to criticism.

Those who were working on this document had three resources
of primary importance before them: The *Apostolic Tradition,* an
early third-century work attributed rightly or wrongly to Hippolytus,[3,1]* the *Gelasian Sacramentary,*[4,2]* and the *Roman Ordo
XI.*[5,3]*

The *Apostolic Tradition* gives us a precise structure for the
catechumenate. It must, however, be seen in the light of its times,
times of raging persecution. In such circumstances there was good
reason to be strict and to give a solid, basic catechesis to the future Christians. Normally, the preparation for the sacraments of
initiation lasts three years. There are a number of supporting
prayers and exorcisms. The candidate's progress is carefully moni-
tored. In fact, there are clear steps along the way towards the
crowning moment of initiation. There is a preliminary examination of the candidate, who is brought forward by his sponsors.
Then he or she begins the catechumenate proper. The catechist
may impose his hands and prayer over the catechumens, either
during the teaching, or if the candidate comes to confide in him
or otherwise is in difficulties.

[3] The *Apostolic Tradition* is a piece of writing from the beginning of the
third century. It has been attributed to St. Hippolytus of Rome. It relates
local liturgical practices which are not necessarily those of the whole city.
Today some scholars think it is a compilation from several hands, or by one
author who may have brought together the various usages.

[4] A sacramentary is a book which contains prayers reserved to the celebrant presiding over the celebration, whether of the Eucharist, or another
sacrament, or of a benediction. The *Gelasian Sacramentary* was not composed by Pope Gelasius (the origin of the name) but it does contain some
elements composed by him. The only manuscript that we possess was written at Chelles, near Paris, in 750. It is conserved in the Vatican Library. The
original would have been composed and written at Rome and copied in France,
and certain practices of the latter country were inserted.

Nevertheless, it remains in essence a Roman document which was to be
used by priests who served the churches of Rome. In the Lateran, the papal
residence, and in its surrounding area a different sacramentary was used,
called the *Gregorian.* Some of the practices it contains date from at least
a century before it was transcribed in France.

[5] *Roman Ordo XI.* An *Ordo* is a book containing information on how
to celebrate. While it is the sacramentary which contains the prayers, the
Ordo indicates the manner of celebrating. Thusly, *Ordo I* describes the Mass
that the pope celebrates on Easter Day at St. Mary Major.

After the time of catechesis has passed, the candidate may be admitted to the preparation leading directly to his or her initiation. This is a second stage, during which there are frequent exorcisms performed over the candidate. He or she then proceeds to the third stage of initiation. The morning before the night when the candidate is to be baptized, the bishop himself performs the exorcism. The rest of the day is spent in fasting and prayer, especially during the long vigil of readings.

At the crowing of the rooster the water is blessed. The baptism is by immersion; first the children are baptized, then the adults, men and women. When it is time to baptize, the bishop consecrates the oil of thanksgiving (holy chrism). The priest has those who are about to be baptized renounce Satan and all his pomps and all his works; next they are anointed with the oil of catechumens. They go down into the font, and the prelate who is to baptize them imposes his hand on the catechumen, asking: "Do you believe in the Father, creator of heaven and earth?" The baptized person answers: "I believe, etc." When he or she comes back out from the font, the priest anoints the person with holy chrism; then, when he or she is dressed, the baptized person goes up to the bishop who pours the chrism onto his or her head and forehead. Then the bishop gives him or her the kiss of peace.

Next begins the preparation of the gifts for the Eucharistic celebration. The ritual of Communion takes place as follows: The bishop gives the consecrated bread with the words: "The bread of heaven in Christ Jesus." The person who receives the bread says: "Amen." The first deacon offers the water, the second the milk and honey, and the third the wine.

This is a summary of what the *Apostolic Tradition* has passed down to us for the catechumenate and initiation itself. Further details could be supplied if there were need.

This ritual influenced subsequent practice. The first witness who gives us precise details on the euchology and the structure of the catechumenate is the *Gelasian Sacramentary*. Actually, a certain John the Deacon passes down to us his comments on these rites somewhat earlier.⁴* We learn that in his day initiation was often conferred upon children of already baptized families. This led to an adaptation: From now on, the catechumen inscribed his or her name on the First Sunday in Lent and then received teaching for three years, as we saw in the *Apostolic Tradition*. Here

John the Deacon shows us that the inscription of the name corresponds to the First Sunday in Lent which provides immediate preparation for the night of Easter, when the catechumen will be baptized.

Through this deacon we learn of the "scrutinies." However, he is misleading when it comes to their meaning. For him, they were examinations of the candidate's knowledge and his or her spiritual qualities in view of the future initiation. His knowledge appears limited to only a part of what the *Apostolic Tradition* teaches us about the interrogating of the catechumen and his sponsors. For those "scrutinies" were mostly exorcisms such as we have in the *Gelasian Sacramentary*.

This sacramentary presents us with three scrutinies, spread out over the Third to the Fifth Sundays in Lent.[5*] It was this structure that our ritual of Christian initiation for adults took over, with certain adaptations. Added to it is a lectionary which probably follows the one used at the moment of the inception of the catechumenate as reported by Gelasian. It corresponds to our Cycle A of Lent. In any parish or community where there are catechumens preparing for baptism during the night of Easter this cycle must be used. This particularly rich series of readings is well known and leads the catechumen through a typological evocation of the sacraments of initiation to his or her sharing in the Pasch of the Lord.

Nevertheless, after hands-on experience with this very beautiful ritual it does seem as if a few corrections could be proposed. We shall organize them into three areas: Adaptation, euchology,[6] and sacramental signs.

The adaptation: Going back to the Gelasian ritual was not done out of an archeological attitude towards liturgy, but out of a recognition of its very real value. Some adaptations were nevertheless made.

It does seem, however, that on at least one point there was some slipping into archaicism. A structure in the Gelasian was copied that was itself already an adaptation of an earlier one.

In fact, the series of "scrutinies" in the Gelasian begins with the Third Sunday in Lent,[6*] and we know the reason: When the

---

[6] Euchology—the law according to which a prayer is composed. The form, structure of the prayer. The prayers of a ritual or a missal considered together.

Ember Days[7] were first introduced, the celebration of Saturday took place at night, with its readings, and Mass was not celebrated on Sunday: The sacramentaries referred to this day by the words *Dominica vacat*.[7]* This was the case for the Second Sunday in Lent, when the Ember Days were introduced in the First week of Lent. We know that in some areas, such as Benevento, for example,[8]* the Gospel reading for the Second Sunday in Lent was the parable of the Good Samaritan. In Rome, the Gospel for the Saturday in Ember Days was the transfiguration.[9]* This reading was assigned to the Second Sunday, when Mass was celebrated on Sunday, and the Saturday in Ember Days was celebrated in the morning. The same Gospel was read on Saturday as Sunday, which was the case in the missal of Pius V. The sermons of St. Leo the Great for Lent assume that the Gospel reading for the Second Sunday in Lent is the transfiguration. But when Mass was not celebrated in this Second Sunday, there were no "scrutinies"; this is the reason why these last were celebrated beginning with the Third Sunday, when the Gospel was that of the Good Samaritan, which related directly to the baptismal "scrutiny." This practice was retained, and there is no reason not to. Nevertheless, we might want to create a celebration for this Second Sunday with the catechumen in mind, since the First Sunday when the catechumen's name is inscribed provides baptismal catechesis and then, suddenly, the second offers nothing.

In fact, it seems that the first two Sundays in Lent provide an outstanding synthesis of the major events in the history of salvation, which the candidate for baptism will soon be experiencing at initiation. On the First Sunday, when the catechumen had his or her name inscribed for baptism, the Church presented the candidate with the full reality of his or her present situation: The Gospel is Genesis 2:7-9 and 3:1-7, in which we read of the creation in unity of the world, but also the Fall of Adam and Eve, which destroyed this unity and the harmony of creation. The can-

[7] Ember Days: These are the Wednesdays, Fridays, and Saturdays of the beginning of the four seasons of the liturgical year that the Church celebrates with abstinence and fasting, and with special readings and Masses. The liturgy for Saturday had six readings before the Epistle and the Gospel. In antiquity, Mass was celebrated in the evening, as a vigil. In that case, there was no assembly on Sunday.

didate must acknowledge this reality. But the Church does not stop at this negative vision of the world; she offers the candidate the vision of Christ's victory over temptation (Matt 4:1-11). The catechumen who had just had his or her name inscribed in order to follow Christ can also overcome evil. The second reading reassures him or her of this: Where sin abounds, there is also abundant grace (Rom 5:12-19). This kind of liturgical and spiritual hermeneutics contains, but also goes beyond, purely exegetical hermeneutics,[8] and gives the catechumen a deep feeling for the goal and the glory of his or her destiny.

And it is precisely this glory that is the subject of the readings for the Second Sunday in Lent. Abraham was called to leave everything behind; after answering the call of the Lord and doing his will, he became a different man and the leader of a people too numerous to count. Christ overcame temptation and gave himself over entirely to the will of his Father and was transfigured in glory. This is the destiny of the Christian who answers his or her vocation. The Lord illumines and transfigures the Christian: This is our holy vocation, and the second reading expresses it well (2 Tim 1:8-10).

So we have here a very beautiful synthesis of the path that lies before the catechumen. Is it not a shame that there is no particular rite or gesture that might express visibly this paschal perspective for the catechumen? There might be room here for creativity; it might be possible to anticipate somewhat and provide the candidate with a candle and an accompanying prayer. One example is suggested here:

---

[8] There are two principal methods of interpretation of the Bible. One is the purely exegetical one, based on history, the comparison of different versions of the text, etc. Second, there is what could be called the "spiritual-exegetical" method which, while respecting fully the strictly exegetical basis of interpretating a text, goes beyond it by also reading into it another meaning, such as a "type" (see note 2). For example, the purely exegetical reading of the story of the Samaritan woman in St. John will not find in the text any intention on the part of the Lord to announce baptism, all the more so that in this story there is no immersion in water, which on the contrary is drunk. Nevertheless, from earliest antiquity the Church and the liturgy have seen in this story a "type" of baptism.

O Lord, our Father, you who will that your Son, having overcome the temptation of the prince of evil, be transfigured, illuminate this catechumen who wishes to answer your call, so that, following the example of your Anointed One, he finds his own transfiguration in you.

The euchology: The ritual for adults attempted, and legitimately so, to adapt the Gelasian formulas. In general they were allowed to remain, but a new prayer was added that was perhaps more easily understood and may also have been more sensitive to the needs of certain mentalities of today; it was hoped also to encourage more active participation. So we have first the ancient prayer for the consecration of the baptismal water, but modified, and then a choice between two new prayers. An advantage of these new prayers is that they provide for acclamations on the part of the faithful, who are thus encouraged to take an active part in the celebration.

The disadvantage, however, is that these prayers have almost nothing to do with the typology of the baptismal water, which is so important, so that the faithful lose the opportunity to learn just what this baptismal water is, avoiding all magical overtones. There is no reason not to introduce here, after each "type" mentioned in the first blessing, an acclamation which would bring the faithful more actively into the act of the consecration of the water. This would kill two birds with one stone: The typology of the baptismal water would be respected, and the faithful would be actively participating.

The sacramental signs: We shall be treating here only of baptism. In the ritual for adults, the three sacraments of Christian initiation are together and in their right order. But we must note the regrettable omission of the post-baptismal anointing, when confirmation follows immediately. What matters is the moment at which the priesthood of the faithful is conferred. (The same holds true of the ritual of confirmation itself, but we shall discuss this later.) Let us take a look at the way in which baptism is conferred upon the adult, as well as First Holy Communion, celebrated with his or her participation, and the crowning experience of initiation.

Baptism: As we saw above in our discussion of the ritual for baptism in the *Apostolic Tradition,* the sacrament is conferred with a triple interrogation to which the catechumen answers: "I believe." We find the same ritual in the Gelasian, and it remains the formula for baptism until around the end of the fifth century, by which time it is mostly children who receive the sacrament. Since the children cannot answer the questions themselves, their sponsors answer for them. It is at this time that the baptismal formula becomes "I baptize you in the name of the Father and of the Son and of the Holy Spirit."

Why not keep the ancient way of baptizing in the case of an adult? There are few enough opportunities for the Christian to take part in the conferring of grace by affirming his or her faith. This may be the result of a narrow theology of the form applied to the matter. It is certainly difficult to dethrone a way of looking at things that we have created ourselves. For we experience no difficulty at all in acknowledging that it is the repeated words of Christ which consecrate, and not a command such as "I consecrate you." We are not motivated by a simple desire to go back to antiquity for its own sake, but by a recognition that this ritual expresses more perfectly the reality of baptism: A gift which responds to the expression of faith.

We shall not go into the question of baptism by immersion, which once again is not mere archeological sentiment, but a return to a ritual which best expresses the meaning of baptism: A birth in water and the Spirit. A few parishes and communities have begun to practice immersion, overcoming obstacles of a practical order, and managing to safeguard the standards of common decency. When we are convinced of the value of an act, of the authenticity of a particular symbolic ritual, we manage to overcome all the obstacles in the way.

Communion: In the ritual of baptism for adults Communion attains its true value in the process of initiation as the crowning experience. But nothing in our present ritual brings out this particular quality of the First Eucharist, whereas it seems fair to say that the first two sacraments are conferred precisely for the purpose of allowing active participation in the reconciliation with God and the rebuilding of a new Covenant through Christ's sacrifice on the cross.

This realization is brought to the fore in the ritual of the *Apostolic Tradition,* where the neophyte is given the Body of Christ, the water, the milk and honey, and then the Blood of

Christ. (The obvious symbolism of the Promised Land scarcely needs to be stressed.) But nothing in our ritual underscores the specific character of this First Eucharist. This bears some reflection. The present author sees no reason why we could not follow the appropriate catechesis with the ritual as found in the *Apostolic Tradition*. It is not a question of nostalgia for antiquity, but of a living catechesis that is the true meaning of Christian initiation in its fullest eschatalogical sense. Bringing this reality more into our ritual is something to which we should give some consideration. We shall be discussing this question further below.

B. Baptism of Children

We do not usually, in our Latin liturgy, speak of the Christian initiation of children. It did exist once, and even as late in some cases as the thirteenth century; but since then the three sacraments of the Christian initiation of children have been separated from one another. For the past fifty years or so, moreover, the highly dubious custom of conferring the Eucharist before confirmation has become general. We shall consecrate a paragraph to this situation as well as to the make-up of the ritual of confirmation itself. We shall be concerned more with the catechesis of the parents than with the ritual of baptism itself, which seems excellent as it is.

The baptismal ritual was well done. In fact, this is the first time that there is an authentic ritual specially adapted for children. Earlier versions were mostly abridgements of the ritual for adults. The child was exorcised three times in the same celebration, copying the ritual for adults, as it was practiced until Vatican II, even though originally the three exorcisms were conferred at three different times. Likewise the euchology has been adapted for a child, who, until now, was given the exorcisms as if he or she were an adult. We shall have a few remarks to make on this topic further on.

a) Catechesis of parents and godparents

The ritual of the baptism of children recommends the catechesis of the parents and those responsible for the Christian education of the child. This catechesis will present differing levels of urgency depending on whether the parents are believers and practicing Christians, or partially believers who do not practice, or whether they are in agreement or not on delegating to responsible parties the Christian education of their child. The ritual does not take these differing cases into account. Nor does it have anything to say about the catechetical method or its supporting framework. It seems useful here to suggest a few ways of handling this situation.

Let us not forget that already the *Gelasian Sacramentary* is in fact written with children in mind, even though certain of its rituals make perfect sense for adults as well, such as the *"traditio"* of the Creed, as well as the *Pater* and the four Gospels. The rubrics leave no doubt about this. At the moment when the Creed is "passed down," we read that the acolyte takes the child on his left arm, and the word is "infans," a child who does not yet talk. This certainly leads us to think that the different *"traditiones"* spoken of are intended for the catechesis of the parents and godparents.[10*]

Moreover, the initiation of infants became quite common at the time of the *Gelasian Sacramentary*. And it is legitimate to use the term "initiation," because it provides for the administration of the three sacraments of initiation one after the other.

It seems moreover that even partially believing and non-practicing parents presented their children for baptism. In fact, *Roman Ordo XI*, which is contemporary with the *Gelasian Sacramentary*, offers a ritual of initiation which is clearly meant for children. The *Gelasian* knows of this ritual; in one of its rubrics it contradicts a rubric in the *Gelasian*, and proves that it is aware of the ritual for children in *Ordo XI*, even though it was composed independently.

So we have here a catechesis meant for parents, and it behooves us to be familiar with it. For the structure which it adopted clearly is addressed to adults; there is no other explanation possible. Not only does it preserve the different "traditions" which only make sense if they are intended for adults, but the different "scrutinies" (that is, as we saw above, a series of exorcisms) go from three to six, not counting the exorcism of Holy Saturday morning. As we see, the number of ceremonies of exorcism has doubled. According to the *Ordo*, the explanation for this is the desire to reach the mystical number of seven. They might also be intended to provide some sort of supplementary insurance, so to speak: Since the infant has no understanding and is entirely passive, doubling the number of exorcisms allows for double the amount of protection. However this may be, it seems certain that what we have here is instruction aimed at the parents, involving them in the progress of their child towards its entry into the Church, and its rebirth.

Could we not see in this material a precedent and important model that can provide inspiration for us today: To adapt and frame in whatever way called for by the circumstances the resources here at our disposal?

We are not speaking of simply copying the ritual in the *Ordo,* but of adapting it more or less. We might even abandon it as it is in the text, but take it as a model to prove that the Church took care to respond to changing needs, as she may wish to do today as well.

Two possibilites are offered here: An *Ordo* for the children of believing parents and another for the children of parents who are not solid in the faith, or who do not believe. Each of these rituals must take into consideration the times when the child is present at the different celebrations and is directly involved, and those times when it is not present, or is not directly involved—in other words, a celebration which concerns the parents exclusively. There is also a choice to be considered, as to whether this same ritual is to be repeated each time a child in the same family is baptized, or whether in that case an abridged form could be used, with the choice left up to the parents.

An *Ordo* for children whose parents are believers: This is in effect a ritual which would be optional, since baptism of the child presents no problems. It does, however, seem important to suggest, at least for the first child, a ritual which encompasses the catechesis of the parents. Since the parents are believers, there doesn't seem to be any particular use in providing for three or four meetings in preparation for baptism. This could, of course, depend on the wishes of the parents.

Ordo XI, which had to find a place in the liturgy for the six exorcisms which it contained, transferred the three exorcisms which belonged respectively to the Third, Fourth, and Fifth Sundays in Lent to weekdays. With that switch, the readings that were assigned to each of the Sundays went along with the exorcisms. The Sundays were then left without assigned readings, and were given those of the days formerly designated for the "scrutinies." In this process all the order and beautiful structure of the Sunday lectionary was completely destroyed. This was the situation which prevailed until the restoration realized by Vatican II. We can judge from this willingness to sacrifice the Sunday lectionary with all its pastoral wealth for the faithful just how great was the importance attached at the time of *Ordo XI* to these multiple exorcisms. The missal of Pius V, the one immediately preceding ours today, bears witness to this loss.

There is no need here to wait for Easter Night—although if it were possible this would be preferable—nor to add on a number of meetings. In one single gathering an exorcism and a "tradition" could be celebrated. This meeting could include the Eucharist, and in this case the exorcism would take place after the homily and the prayer of the faithful, while the "traditions" could be assigned to a meeting for the inscribing of a name or an exorcism. These meetings could consist of a Liturgy of the Word alone. The readings would be those of Cycle A.

The inscription of the name would take place during the first meeting, with the readings from Cycle A and their catechetical homily. It would be a simple ritual. After the proclamation of the Gospel and the homily, the name would be inscribed. The celebrant has opened the parish register upon the altar. The parents come forward, and after the celebrant has asked them: "What name do you wish to give to your child?" and, "What do you seek for your child?" he writes the name in the register, and the parents write their signature next to the name. This meeting is clearly catechetical in purpose. The presiding clergy comments on Genesis 2:7-9, and 3:1-7. He explains God's creative plan conceived out of love for humankind and his divine will to open a dialogue with his people. Then he goes on to describe the sin and the Fall of our first parents, which weigh upon each child born thereafter. But through the faith of these parents and of the Church, baptism will readmit the child to the Covenant.

But we should like to propose a somewhat meatier ritual in the eventuality that the Congregation for Divine Worship may some day see the possibility of moving in the direction suggested here. We would like to offer a generous number of possibilities, while emphasizing that they are only given as possible examples.

At the first meeting, then, when the name of the child is inscribed, the catechesis comments on the readings for the first Sunday in Cycle A, which concern sin and the grace of baptism which brings reconciliation.

Could we not consider this as a valued precedent and a useful model for us to draw on today? Some reworking and adapting to varying needs would, of course, need to be done.

It is not suggested that the *Ordo* be copied slavishly, but adapted as seen fit. It could even be altogether abandoned, but its existence could be used to show the will of the Church at a particular point in time to respond to a specific situation, such as, perhaps, we have today.

Therefore, we can conceive of two possibilities: An *Ordo* for the children of Christian parents, and another for the children of parents who are not fully believers, or are non-believers. Each of these rituals should take into account the times when the child may be present and involved to some degree, and those when he or she is not present, or is not directly involved. In this latter case, we would be creating a ritual with the parents in mind.

The question also arises whether the same ritual should be repeated for each child born to the same couple, or whether an abbreviated ritual might not be an option for the parents.

b) An Ordo *for the children of Christian parents*

It should be pointed out that such a ritual would be purely optional in this case, since the baptism of already converted parents presents no problem. Nevertheless, it would seem of value to provide a ritual with some catechetical value for the parents, especially in the case of the baptism of the first child. Here we would not propose more than three or four preparatory meetings before the baptism. This number could of course be increased if, for instance, the parents so desired.

In the case of the baptism of a child, *Ordo XI* shows a preference for spacing the exorcisms out over a period of time. This would allow for the catechesis of the parents to benefit from experiencing the progress of their child towards full participation in the life of the Church. This is the practice that we would like to see implemented. However, if the Church authorities should not permit this, nor even give the local bishop the authority to allow it, then we propose yet another formula.

1) THE *Ordo* OF THE CATECHESIS OF THE PARENTS AND THE
EXORCISMS OF THE CHILD

At the beginning of the celebration, the presiding clergy offers
a warm welcome to the parents and godparents. Then, the celebration of the Word begins. At the end of the catechesis, the priest
has the parents come to the altar and asks them what name they
wish to give to their child. He writes the name with all solemnity
into the register which lies on the altar, and he has the parents
sign their own names next to that of their child. Then he inter-
rogates the parents:

"You therefore are asking for the Faith for your child. Are
you ready to show your child a good example and to guide him
on his way to God in the Church?" They answer: "We are ready."
"And you, godfathers and godmothers, are you also prepared
to help this child to seek Christ?" Answer: "We are prepared to
help him." The celebrant then prays over the parents, the godparents, and the child:

**Most merciful Father, we give you thanks for these parents and
godparents who are ready to guide this child to your Son. They
accept the responsibility to prepare themselves in prayer and
meditation in order better to fulfill their role. We praise you
and bless you for these parents and godparents.**

He goes over to the child and marks his forehead and sense
organs as is possible with the sign of the cross. Then he says:

**Receive the cross on your forehead. May Christ himself pro-
tect you with this sign of his love and his victory. May your
parents, godfathers, and godmothers teach you to know Christ
and follow him.**

(If he traces the sign of the cross on the child's sense organs,
he can draw on the prayers in the ritual for adults that accompany each one of these gestures.)

Then the priest turns to the parents and the child and says:
"The name of your child is therefore _____. May his patron
saint keep this child in the path of the true life."

Next he says the following prayer:

**Almighty God, who through the cross and the resurrection of
your Son have given life to your people, grant this child who**

has received the sign of the cross the grace to follow you, to listen to the teaching of his parents, and to imitate their example.

Then the parents and godparents go to the altar, and the priest gives them a book containing the four Gospels, as he says:

Receive this book of the Gospels; read it with respect and draw from it the holy doctrine which you will later present through your living of it to this child.

Lastly comes the prayer of the faithful, in which the assembly prays for the child, his parents, and his godparents.

The theme of the second meeting will be taken from the Third Sunday of Cycle A, which has to do with water (Exod 17:3-7; Rom 5:1-2, 8; John 4: 5-42). The homily will explain how Christ came to make all things new. He changed water into wine, he announced the birth of the new man to Nicodemus, born of water and the Spirit; he tells the Samaritan woman of the water which will quench all thirst forever, he announces a new temple, he and we together, a new religion where the rituals correspond to an actual reality.

After the homily and the prayer of the faithful which takes up the theme of the readings and prays for the child, the parents, and godparents, the celebrant proceeds to the first exorcism over the child, saying:

Lord Jesus, you are he who renews all things by your grace. Give to this child to receive the living water, given to the Samaritan woman in the Gospel. May this child be transformed by your word, by water and the Spirit. Take away from him all trace of evil, make of him the temple of your Spirit, that he may give you glory.

At the third meeting, the readings and catechesis will concentrate on the theme of light, received in baptism. The readings will be those of the Fourth Sunday in Lent, Cycle A. The first reading, 1 Samuel 16:4, 6-7, 10-13, presents the theme of being chosen by God: David is chosen to be king over his brothers, who were, from a human point of view, more likely to have become king. The baptized is anointed like a king and receives the light which allows him to judge things correctly and to know the mysteries of God (John 9:1-41). He is illumined; as such, it behooves him to live as a son of the light—brought back from the dead, Christ brings him light (Eph 5:8-14).

After the homily and an appropriate prayer of the faithful, the celebrant goes over to the child for the second exorcism. He stretches out his hands over him and says:

> **Father most kind, you gave faith in Christ your Son to the man born blind and gave him a place in your kingdom. Give to this child whom you have chosen to be free of all false beliefs and to grow into a strong man of faith. May he become a son of the light and radiate holiness and grace. Through Christ our Lord.**

At the end of this third meeting, the celebrant might offer an interpretation of the *Credo* for the benefit of the parents and god-parents, reminding them that the gift of the Holy Spirit which they received at confirmation has illumined their faith. For this "*traditio*" of the *Credo,* the following outline could be used: The celebrant addresses the parents and godparents:

> **Dearly beloved, listen to the words of faith, which have given you a new life and will give a new life to this child. The words are few, but they are rich in the mysteries of God. Hear them, and keep them in your hearts in order to be able to teach them, in love, to this child.**

The celebrant then begins the *Credo,* which is then recited by the assembly. A brief commentary follows. Then he invites all present to pray with him. After a moment of silence he says:

> **O Lord, source of light and truth, we look to your mercy for this child here today. Open his mind to the teachings of the Church, and may he listen to the instruction of his parents, god-fathers, and godmothers when they teach him the rudiments of the faith which leads them to your kingdom. Through Christ our Lord.**

At the fourth meeting the theme is resurrection and life. The readings are those of the Fifth Sunday in Lent, Cycle A. This is the high point of initiation. The child is about to receive the gift of everlasting life, a resurrected life with Christ.

As usual, the Liturgy of the Word is followed by a homily and then the prayer of the faithful. Then the celebrant proceeds to the third exorcism of the child, stretching out his hands over the child and saying:

> **O God, Father of eternal life, you are the God of the living and not of the dead. You sent your Son to bring the message of life in order to free men from the kingdom of death and to bring them to the resurrection. Free this child from all power of evil, and may he receive new life with Christ resurrected. He who lives and reigns forever and ever.**

After this the celebrant enjoins the *Pater* upon the parents and godparents (this could be done at the same time as the *Credo*). For the *traditio* of the *Pater*, the celebrant says: "Hear how the Lord taught his disciples to pray."

He proclaims Matthew 6:9-13 and emphasizes the importance of prayer, which the parents should teach to the child very early in life.

For the other rites, the ritual for the baptism of children can be used.

In the above ritual, even while the parents and godparents are being catechized, they are involved in the introduction of their child into Christian life. So we are not making any innovations here, but actually are carrying out the prescriptions of *Ordo XI,* which provided for six meetings and a seventh one the Saturday morning before the baptism. What we have proposed above corresponds to this schema, while adapting it to present-day needs.

2) Catechesis of the Parents without Exorcisms of the Child

It is possible that these exorcisms of the child are not permitted, or that it seems better to leave them out for judicious reasons, such as, for instance, the fear that they may be given a magical interpretation by some of the family of the child. In such a case the catechesis of the parents can be limited to a Liturgy of the Word, with catechesis, the *traditio* of the Creed, the Gospels, and the *Pater.*

How should the liturgical setting of this catechesis be organized? Let us not forget that the previous schema with the spread-out exorcisms of the child requires prior study and the approval of the Congregation for Divine Worship. In fact, these suggestions were intended only as the object of further study. However, when it comes to developing a simple catechetical setting, no authorization is needed. Still, is would be best for any such suggestions to be at least made known to the liturgical commission of the diocese.

The first meeting entails the inscription of the child's name. Catechesis is provided in the homily after the Liturgy of the Word. The readings are those of the First Sunday in Lent, Cycle A. As a symbolic gesture, the parents will sign their names in the register where the celebrant has written the name of their child. A prayer could be recited here concerning both the child and his parents.

After the catechesis, the appropriate prayer of the faithful, and the inscription of the child's name, the celebrant says:

> **Lord, you who created human beings in your almighty power and who in your great mercy have redeemed them, look down upon the child of these parents who have pronounced the name that will be given their child in baptism. Protect this child and give his parents the grace to prepare themselves in faith for the celebration of his baptism, and to understand fully their duty to lead him to you on the path of an education according to your will. Through Jesus Christ your Son, our Lord.**

At the second meeting, the Liturgy of the Word will present the readings of the Second Sunday in Lent, Cycle A. Like Abraham, the parents have been called by the Lord to be children of God. The Lord, through them, calls their child to divine life (first reading, Gen 12:1-4). All the baptized are so called—it is their holy vocation (second reading, 2 Tim 1:8-10) to be transfigured with Christ who has triumphed over evil (Matt 17:1-9).

A catechetical homily of some length should be given on the subject of these passages. After an appropriate prayer of the faithful, the celebrant prays:

> **Lord, you called our fathers to the faith and you have given us the grace to have our way illumined by the Gospel. Keep these parents on your path and may they prepare themselves to raise their child by guiding him towards his transfiguration. Through Christ our Lord.**

Next the celebrant entrusts the Gospel to the parents, giving them the book while saying:

> **Receive the Gospel of Jesus Christ the Son of God; fill yourselves with its doctrine and its examples, in order to be able to nourish your child with them, and to teach him to follow its precepts.**

At the third meeting the Liturgy of the Word emphasizes the theme of the waters of baptism, using the readings of the Third Sunday in Lent, Cycle A. The catechesis of these passages is simple, but loses nothing of the richness contained in these readings. Here is the prime opportunity to develop the typology of water, starting with the first blessing of the baptismal water, and comparing it with the waters of Creation, the water of the Flood, the water of the Red Sea, the water of the rock at Horeb (first reading), the waters of the Jordan, the water changed into wine at Cana (John 2), the rebirth of water and the Spirit (John 3), the water of Jacob's well and the well of the Samaritan woman (the Gospel of the day, John 4) with the new temple and the new cult. This new man, the baptized child, will become the temple of the new cult, and the Spirit will be poured out into his heart (second reading).

After a homily rich in catechesis and the prayer of the faithful, the celebrant will say the following prayer:

> **Lord, you have sent your Son to make all things new, with your Holy Spirit. Let these parents who were reborn in their baptism find the strength to hand down to their child, whom you will make into a new person born of water and the Spirit, the faith that they have received from you. Through Christ our Lord.**

The celebrant then gives the creed of the Apostles to the parents and speaks to them thusly: "The realities that you have just heard are held in the faith of the Church. In order to strengthen your faith that you will transmit to your child, let us recite together the *Credo*." When the Symbol of the Apostles has been proclaimed, the celebrant says the following prayer:

> **Lord, you are the source of light and truth. We ask your mercy upon these parents who are preparing for the baptism of their**

child. Give them the light and the strength of faith, so that they may be able to hand it down with love and faithfulness to the child whom Divine Providence has willed to come forth of their flesh, and whom you are bringing forth into new birth through water and the Spirit. Through Jesus Christ our Lord.

In the fourth celebration the theme of the Liturgy of the Word is light, following the readings of the Fourth and Fifth Sundays in Lent, Cycle A. If possible, it would be best to keep the readings of the Fifth Sunday for a fifth meeting, but if it seems desirable to limit the number of meetings, the themes of the two readings can be combined: The illumination of the baptized, chosen like David to be king along with Christ triumphant and resurrected in glory.

After the catechesis and the appropriate prayer of the faithful, the celebrant will recite this prayer:

Lord our God, you who have chosen us to be illumined by your Spirit and to share in your resurrection, give ever more light to these parents, so that, for their child's sake, the glory of your resurrection shines through them. Through the same Jesus Christ our Lord.

The celebrant then enjoins the *Pater* upon the parents, introducing it with these words:

Let us recite together the prayer that Jesus taught us. As adopted brothers of Jesus Christ we have truly a right to say "our Father." May the kingdom of the Father come through us, and may this prayer of Jesus be the first that you as parents teach to your child.

The meeting will end with the following prayer:

Almighty and eternal God, give us ever greater understanding of our faith, and may this child who will soon be reborn into new life be welcomed among your adopted sons, and may he say in all truth: Our Father. Through your Son, Jesus, our Lord.

3) THE *Ordo* FOR THE CATECHESIS OF PARENTS WHO ARE NOT FULLY BELIEVERS, FOR THE BAPTISM OF THEIR CHILD

It is by no means rare, in Europe as well as in more recently Christianized countries, for parents who are not fully believers themselves to ask that their child be baptized. Their motives may be quite complex, ranging from a sense of benefit for their child that they do not want to lose, to a sort of sheer superstition. It would not be appropriate to categorically deny baptism in these cases, but it could be put off, with the explanation that the Church cares about them, the parents, but that, out of respect for the persons of the parents, she does not wish to baptize a child unless someone will shoulder the responsibility of raising the child in the faith. Either the parents delegate this responsibility to some other persons, who then will receive appropriate catechesis as described above, or else the parents elect to accept this responsibility themselves. In this latter case, one explains to them the necessity of receiving a catechesis which prepares them for their responsibility in this baptism. Two possibilities exist: A catechesis which involves the step-by-step preparation of their child for baptism through the successive exorcisms, or a catechesis in a liturgical setting without the presence of the child, and without the exorcisms. Whereas the permission of the proper authorities is necessary for the first, the second needs no such permission, although it is undoubtedly a good idea for its celebration to be cleared with the liturgical commission of the diocese.

4) A CATECHESIS FOR THE PARENTS AND FOR THE EXORCISMS OF THE CHILD

It is not possible at this point to follow *Ordo XI,* which is too much under the influence of its time, not only in its ritual, but also in its euchology. New celebrations must be created. Clearly, whatever we propose here is by way of suggestions for further work, if indeed it seems desirable to think along the lines we propose, which the present author does find desirable and of importance for our times.

A first meeting would use the texts of the First Sunday in Lent of Cycle A. The entire catechesis should treat of these realities which explain the reason for Christian initiation and its fruits.

At the end of the catechesis, the homily, and a prayer of the faithful which speaks to this particular case, the celebrant turns to the parents and says:

> **Dear parents, when you ask for baptism for your child, you are promising solemnly to raise him in the faith, so that he may**

learn by keeping the commandments to love God and his neighbor, as Christ taught us.

May I ask you if you are fully aware of your responsibility, and are not motivated by secondary considerations, such as the desire for some advantage, or the wish to please your families and preserve their customs?

Then he turns to the godparents (who must in every case be approved by the priest who will perform the baptism, and must be present at this celebration) and says: "Are you ready to help these parents fulfill such an important responsibility?"

Then the celebrant has the parents come to the altar. He asks the parents: "What name have you chosen to give to this child?" He writes the name in the register which is upon the altar, and the parents sign their names next to that of their child.

The celebrant then says: "This name which has just been inscribed in this register is also inscribed in heaven."

He then goes to the child and makes the sign of the cross on his forehead, saying:

We joyfully receive N. _____ into our Christian community, and it is in the name of this community that I have just made the sign of the cross on the forehead of this child. Parents and godparents, will you now please also make the sign of the cross on the forehead of N. _____ .

The celebrant gives a book containing the Gospels to the parents, saying:

Receive these Gospels; they are the law of Christ. Open them, learn from them, for the strengthening of your faith, in order to be able to teach them to your child.

Then he warmly welcomes the parents and godparents and teaches them how to perform a baptism in the case of an emergency. He also explains to them that even if the child were to die without having received the sacrament of baptism, he would still be saved. Future meeting times are agreed upon for the catechesis preparatory to baptism, which will take place when the priest judges that the parents are sufficiently prepared.

If the time of preparation turns out to be somewhat lengthy, the priest, the catechists, and even the godparents with proper guidance could recite prayers of blessing over the child, so long as it is well understood that these prayers have no magical power and do not constitute a sacrament. A blessing over the parents could also be said. We offer the following by way of suggestion:

> **Lord, bless these parents who are being instructed in the Gospel of your Christ. Lead them to know and love you, and prepare them to fulfill your will. Bless this child whom you have chosen to be among your adopted sons, in your Son, Jesus, our Lord.**

Or:

> **Lord, through the coming of your Son you have freed the world from error. Hear our prayer and give these parents a solid understanding of the faith and profound knowledge of the truth. Let their child soon receive the grace of being sanctified in the water of baptism.**

When a date for the baptism is agreed upon, approximately three weeks ahead of time the immediate preparation of the child and the parents will be set up, including the three scrutinies and the *traditio* of the creed of the faith and the *Pater*.

At this point the celebration continues as above, in the catechesis of parents who are believers.

As we have said repeatedly, these suggestions are only that, and are intended to raise questions in the hope of some eventual resolution. It seems that with the evident diminution of the quality of faith in our day that it is not enough simply to baptize children; we must also provide careful preparation both in catechetical teaching and in the liturgical setting so that parents and godparents derive the most sustenance possible from the celebration of the sacrament.

We have been concentrating mostly on supplementing the ritual of baptism of children itself, attempting to provide a liturgical framework leading up to the conferring of the sacrament.

But this does not mean that there is no room for improvement in the ritual itself. A few remarks may be permitted here, which fall under three general headings: (1) an unnecessary number of interrogations; (2) a somewhat defective euchology; (3) the excessive repetition of the same acts.

c) An unnecessary number of interrogations

There are about a dozen interrogations. One gets the impression that those who drew up this ritual were in some sense responding to objections which were disturbing to them, as, for instance, the questioning of the legitimacy of baptizing a child. The truly excessive number of questionings gives an impression of uneasiness, which ultimately is quite offensive for those who must answer. At the very beginning of the celebration, the parents and godparents are asked if they are fully aware of the grave responsibility they are undertaking. Then as the ritual leads on through the various questions to the act of renunciation and the promises of baptism, their responsibility to educate the child in the faith is again insistently enjoined. Again, just before conferring baptism, the parents are interrogated as to their will to have their child baptized. When the child has been clothed in the white garment, the parents are once more asked to take care for the education of their child and to remain persevering in the faith. During the last blessing the parents are asked to be the primary witnesses to the faith for their child, in both word and deed.

The reasons for this insistence are readily understandable. But must it be pushed to such an obsessive level? The ritual can become somewhat embarrassing, although the celebrant can soften the effect by not giving the same emphasis to each of the repeated interrogatons and reminders of responsibility. The overall effect is not one of celebration.

One group of questions is particularly offensive: those which constantly harp on the assuming of responsibility on the part of the parents and godparents. Another group concerns the authenticity of the sacrament about to be conferred. There is, of course, a serious purpose to these interrogations, but it is perhaps a shame that they are so numerous in what is, after all, a very brief celebration.

d) A somewhat defective euchology

The euchology is not entirely above criticism either, particularly in the exorcism and in the blessing of the water. New exorcisms have been created out of necessity. It was not possible to exorcise a child with the same wordings as an adult. The challenge was to soften the formulas without losing the essence of the rite.

Eventually the exorcism was presented in four parts, which seems somewhat overdone. A simple reading of the ritual reveals the lack of unity in the prayers, and the resulting weakening of their impact.

Certain criticisms have already been made of the choice of blessings of the water during our discussion of the ritual for adults, in order to bring out more clearly the biblical typology of water.

e) Excessive repetition of the same acts

The ritual calls for five distinct places where people move about. The first is the procession of the celebrant and his assistants who go to the church entrance while a psalm or appropriate hymn is sung. Then there is a procession accompanied by song to the place where the Liturgy of the Word is to be celebrated. Next, there is a procession to the baptismal font. After the baptism, the assembly processes to the altar for the recitation of the *Pater*. And finally there is a procession to the altar of the Blessed Virgin. For the space of fifteen to twenty minutes this is just too much. Moreover, the more often an action is repeated, the more it loses in significance for those involved. Two processions would be sufficient: one to the baptismal font and the other to the altar for the celebration of the Eucharist, which is the high point of the initiation.

C. Confirmation

This sacrament is a delicate topic, both in terms of its theology and its pastoral aspects.

Scripture, in fact, says very little about this sacrament. Even the commentaries of the Fathers of the Church make only meager mention of it. In their day, confirmation always followed immediately upon baptism and preceded the Eucharist. Since it had little scriptural foundation, it was difficult to develop a theology of the sacrament, which was then free to evolve in different ways in different Churches and regions. The *magisterium* of the Church limited itself to declaring that confirmation is a sacrament instituted by Christ, but there is no dogma on the subject. From a pastoral point of view, the practice of the sacrament has varied a great deal and has not always been clearly justified.

It seems necessary to give these points some thought, especially since the new ritual of confirmation created after Vatican II presents some knotty problems.

The present author has, upon various occasions, attempted to address some of these considerations. Some previously published material will be offered here, either in their entirety or in part, depending on the light that they shed on this subject.

a) *Theological and pastoral aspects*
(The gift of the Spirit in confirmation—the giving of the Spirit, the activity of the Spirit)

No one has ever questioned the fact that confirmation confers the Holy Spirit. But not everyone understands just how this takes place in the same way, nor is there unanimity on the nature of the fruits of the Spirit's intervention.

For centuries the prayer to the Father that accompanies the imposition of the hand or the hands on the confirmands both in the past and in the new *Ordo* mentions specifically the seven gifts of the Spirit, according to the prophecy of Isaiah that is applied to the Holy Spirit. The new *Ordo* of confirmation emphasizes the gift of the Spirit in confirmation. The new prayer accompanying the anointing is quite precise, although it is essential that the text be correctly understood.

There do arise, nevertheless, a few questions which, up to now, have not been satisfactorily answered. The Spirit is, of course, "given" in confirmation. Without "reifying" this gift of the Spirit, can one ask whether this gift is specific to the sacrament of confirmation and perhaps to holy orders as well, or whether one can speak of the gift of the Spirit in all the sacraments?

Where St. Matthew gives us the words of Christ when he sends out the apostles to announce the kingdom and to baptize (28:18-19), the verses touching on baptism do not speak of the gift of the Spirit, but of the insertion of the newly baptized into the Father, the Son, and the Holy Spirit. We should not read a liturgical formula into this text, nor was it used as such before the sixth century in the Roman Church. But "baptizing in the Father, the Son, and the Spirit" certainly implies the efficacity of the sacrament of baptism, which brings the baptized into the life of the Trinity. He or she is born of water and the Spirit and becomes a new person, through the activity of the Holy Spirit.

In the apostolic community baptism by water is conferred in the name of Jesus (Acts 2:28; 10:48; 19:5; 22:16; cf. 1 Cor 1:13-16; 6:11; Gal 3:27; Rom 6:3).

Other passages in Acts used the noun *donum* (2:38; 10:45), and the verbs *dare, accipere Spiritum Sanctum* for a mission involving the imposition of the hands (8:15-19; 19:2).

Of course, this is all very elementary, and a serious exegetical study along these lines is called for. Still, one can even now ask some questions about the meaning of this word "gift" of the Spirit. Even while it is admitted that it cannot represent anything material like a "present," should it perhaps be reserved for those times when the candidate is to be sent on a mission, as in confirmation and holy orders? Even while it is recognized that the Spirit acts in all the sacraments (in baptism, where it transforms man into a new creature; and in the Eucharist, where it transforms the bread into the Body of Christ in order to transform those who eat it), is it not possible that the Spirit is more specifically "given" in the two sacraments which entrust a mission to the candidate?

Tertullian speaks to this point when he writes, concerning baptism: "It is not in the water that we receive the Spirit, but in the water, which is purified by the angel, we are prepared to receive the Spirit."[13]*

Moreover, the Council of Trent declared anathema anyone who denies that the Holy Spirit is "given" in the sacrament of holy orders.[14]*

What we need to know is what is meant by the word "given." The text of Tertullian is quite clear on this point, but the same cannot be said for the statement of Trent, where "given" could be understood just as well as "acting."

The first question which theologians need to address is, therefore, whether one should say that the Spirit is "given" as a gift in each of the sacraments. And if the answer is yes, should it be specified that in some sacraments the gift is an action, and that in others it is an action which is specifically preparing the one who receives it for a mission?

A precise answer is important, even if the sacraments are not to be distinctly separated one from the other, or even if we should emphasize the unity of the sacraments of Christian initiation as being one sacrament in three sacramental stages. It is, in fact, precisely at this point that the Spirit can be seen as transforming human beings into new men and women in baptism, as charging them with their mission in confirmation, and as making them actors in the New Covenant in the Eucharist.

1) THE SPECIFICITY OF THE GIFT OF THE SPIRIT IN CONFIRMATION

Most often confirmation is understood as the gift of the Spirit which prepares the faithful to bear witness and to have the strength for trials ahead.

If this is the accepted theology, there is no longer any particular importance in establishing the exact place of confirmation in its relationship to the Eucharist, for example. It is a sacrament *in se stante,* which confers strengthening and is linked to the act of bearing witness.

It is on this basis that certain pastoral practices have come into being, such as putting off as long as possible the conferring of confirmation and administering the sacrament of the Eucharist before confirmation. For these reasons it seems important to be more specific about the nature of the gift of the Spirit in confirmation. One option open to us is to study the thought of the ancient Church authorities. Only a few excerpts can be given here.

At the beginning of the third century, the *Apostolic Tradition,* attributed right or wrongly to Hippolytus of Rome, gives us the euchology which, at least within its sphere of influence, accompanied the imposition of the hand by the bishop on the head of the confirmand:

> Lord God, you who have made them worthy of the forgiveness of sins through the bath of rebirth, make them worthy to be filled with the Holy Spirit and send your grace down upon them, so that they may serve you according to your will. . . .[15]*

For baptism and the forgiveness of the sins of the baptized, there is no mention of the "gift" of the Spirit in any of the Eastern versions of the text, Arabic, Boairic, or Ethiopian.

The Latin version attributes the forgiveness of sins to the *lavacrum regenerationis Spiritus Sancti.* Hippolytus speaks of inviting into the Faith in the "intervention" of the Spirit in the act of baptism, but does not mention any "gift" of the Spirit.

Quite the contrary, in the case of the confirmands, he considers them "filled" with the Holy Spirit. The Spirit is given for its own sake, and not for purposes of transforming the confirmed, as in baptism; what is stressed is not the confirmed, but what is to "come out of" them.

But the phrase at the ending of Hippolytus' prayer seems important to us. The gift of the Spirit is sought: ". . . ut tibi serviant secundum voluntatem tuam" ("that they may serve you, according to your will"). It is easy to see the Johannine influence here to which Hippolytus would conceivably have been exposed through the works of Irenaeus of Lyons: A number of passages prove that he was very familiar with these last.

In several places in the *Apostolic Tradition,* we read the word *servire,* usually in a liturgical context. One example among many other similar ones, on the subject of the ordination of a bishop: ". . . et sanctum tuum sine ministeri non derelinquens" ("the sanctuary must not be without caretaking").[16]* The bishop must: ". . . primatum sacerdotii tibi exhibere sine repraehensione, servientem noctu et die" ("the bishop must serve day and night in prayer").[17]* In the Eucharistic prayer that Hippolytus suggests as a model for a recently ordained bishop who is celebrating for the first time with his diocese, we read in the Latin version: ". . . quia nos dignos habuisti adstare coram te et tibi ministrare" ("for you have judged us worthy of standing before you and serving you").[18]* For the ordination of a deacon, the prayer asks that God make him worthy to serve him and to give him praise, and it recalls that Christ was sent to serve according to the will of God.

So the theme of service is frequently identified with liturgical service, along with service as doing the will of God.

In order to fulfill this service the confirmand receives the gift of the Spirit, and he is "filled" with it.

Further on, one particular instruction which is rarely commented on seems of importance here: After the bishop has anointed the confirmed and given him or her the kiss of peace, Hippolytus notes: "Et postea iam simul cum omni populo orent, non primum orantes cum fidelibus, nisi omnia haec fuerint consecuti" ("they cannot pray with the faithful before having received the preceding").[19]* This is a significant remark which shows beyond a doubt that, for Hippolytus, confirmation enables the confirmed to take part in the liturgy.

Moving quickly through the centuries, it may be of interest to note what St. Thomas Aquinas has to say. In one place he writes that confirmation acts as the sacrament which gives the strength to announce the Passion of Christ,[20]* but in a number of other passages he embellishes his theological vision, and we read in the *Summa Theologica*:

> Through baptism man is invested with the power to receive the other sacraments: This is why baptism is called the gate to all the other sacraments. In a certain way confirmation also disposes to the same thing, that is, to worship.[21]*

St. Thomas also speaks of the close relationship between confirmation and holy orders. Both prepare for a particular role in the Church:

> We must say that for holy orders and confirmation the faithful of Christ are designated certain particular roles (duties, activities) which concern their role as leader (*officium principis?*).[22]*

Even though the exact meaning of *officium principis* is not clear, what interests us is the parallel between confirmation and holy orders. The specific character of the gift of the Spirit in confirmation, if we read the preceding passages, seems to go beyond the conferring of the ability to bear witness.

Going back a little in time: when St. Cyprian of Carthage calls the sacrament of confirmation *consummatio,* and when St. Ambrose of Milan writes: "Post fontem remanet perfectio" ("after the font remains the perfecting"),[23]* do we not have here a specific gift which confers a perfect conforming to Christ? Indeed, this is confirmed in the Consitution *Divinum consortium naturae,* which introduces our contemporary ritual for confirmation. Moreover, this is what is said clearly in *Lumen Gentium* on the subject of the priesthood of the faithful.[24]* This is what is expressed today in the formula accompanying the anointing after baptism by the priest. All of this leads us to pursue further our reflections on the specificity of the gift of the Spirit in confirmation.

2) Is there a sacrament which confers priesthood on the faithful?

When St. Leo the Great, on the occasion of the fourth anniversary of his consecration as bishop of Rome, speaks to the Christians who have come to pay him homage, he explains to them how all the baptized have received the gift of the Spirit, which makes them priests. If the anointing was done at somewhat more length in his case, so that he could render his service to the Church, nevertheless all the faithful have received this anointing. When they come to honor him for the anniversary of his consecration, they are really honoring themselves.[25]*

This beautiful text could hardly be more explicit. According to St. Leo, a sacramental act has conferred priesthood upon the Christian faithful. He makes no apparent distinction between the anointing right after baptism and the anointing of confirmation. If we read Hippolytus, then Cyprian, and finally Ambrose, it seems to be confirmation that is meant.

But our *Ordines* of Christian initiation designate baptism as conferring this priesthood of the faithful. In fact, having enriched a sacramental liturgy with the express and unmistakable power of conferring the priesthood of the faithful is something new. The *Praenotanda* (prefatory remarks) declare: "Chrismatis unctio post Baptismum significat sacerdotium regale baptizatorum. . . ."

In order to underscore this reality, Ambrose added a very meaningful formula to the liturgy of this anointing in the *De sacramentis:* "God, the almighty Father, who has made you to be reborn of water and the Spirit and who has forgiven you your sins, anoints you himself unto eternal life."[26]*

The *Gelasian Sacramentary,* which was followed by all our rituals until Vatican II, presents the following text, almost identical to the preceding:

> Almighty God, Father of our Lord Jesus Christ, who has made you to be reborn of water and the Spirit and who has forgiven you your sins, anoints you himself with the chrism of salvation, in Jesus Christ our Savior, unto eternal life.[27]*

Our present ritual, following its own introduction, which specifies that baptism confers priesthood upon the faithful, adds:

> . . . anoints you himself with the chrism of salvation, so that, ordained priest, prophet, and king in the midst of the people of Christ you shall be forever a member of this people, for eternal life.[28]*

Introducing thus the priesthood of the faithful into the prayer accompanying the anointing right after baptism has been made specific only in modern times. Clearly, it has its practical reasons inasmuch as it justifies the practice which is usual now in the Latin Church of conferring the Holy Eucharist upon those who have not yet been confirmed. If priesthood has already been conferred upon the faithful at his or her baptism, this practice is legitimate. But in that case, confirmation is an isolated entity and does not lead up to any other sacrament. It is the sacrament of strengthening, of witnessing. It becomes a sort of crowning experience of initiation, whereas it is obvious that it is the Eucharist that holds this primary position.

This significant introduction into the prayer, found already in Ambrose at the moment of the post-baptismal anointing, has some basis in the patristic writings. However, we must recognize that the exact meaning of these texts which speak of this gift of the Spirit in baptism is not as clear as might seem at first.

First, when the Fathers use the term "baptism," they are referring to the totality of the experience of a Christian initiation, and not specifically just to baptism proper.

Still, there are many texts of the Fathers which do mean specifically baptism and speak of the gift of the Spirit. But here we must be careful not to base ourselves on the Greek Fathers, for whom the postbaptismal anointing is our confirmation. We must take into consideration here only the Fathers of the Latin Church, who speak of the imposition of the hands by the bishop after the baptismal anointing, followed by the signing with chrism, this time by the bishop. Among the ecclesiastical writers of the Latin Church there are, undeniably, some who comment upon the postbaptismal anointing and see in it the conferring of the priesthood of the faithful. But the exact meaning of some of these texts is open to question and may well refer to the anointing of confirmation.

We shall not attempt an exegesis here of these texts, but we feel that they should be looked at again, and a deeper study of them made. Another point should be kept in mind, namely, that the homiletic language used may, at times, and seemingly consciously, raise certain questions. Tertullian, as we have seen, declares explicitly that the gift of the Spirit does not reside in the water, but rather that the water predisposes to receiving it. Yet the same writer does not hesitate in other of his writings seemingly to contradict himself, when he speaks of the seal of faith in baptism as being a gift of the Spirit.

Moreover, there would be no reason not to see in baptism a first gift of the Spirit, followed by a second in confirmation. In this case, the purpose of the gift should not be seen as restricted to the strengthening of the faithful and his or her preparation to bear witness, but should include being sent forth to announce the kingdom, and to realize in the sacraments that which is announced; the Eucharist itself being the sacramental announcing of the Pasch.

But our present-day *Ordo* of confirmation, as we have seen above, insists on the gift of priesthood of the faithful in baptism, to the extent of having interpolated the text of the ancient prayer, transmitted by St. Ambrose. As far as we know, no known ritual includes any such explicit statement in its rites or its formulas. Ambrose, moreover, would not have emphasized this priesthood conferred by baptism in the postbaptismal prayer, for it was he who called confirmation the sacrament of "perfection" (completeness). In other words, it is confirmation which gives the faithful their completed likeness to Christ, whose supreme characteristic is that of Priest, he who has offered and continues to offer his sacrifice, with which we have become associated, and even more, assimilated.

Now, at the moment when our ritual, with some audacity, proclaims alone among all the others the priestly dignity of the baptized, it introduces an astonishing rubric: If confirmation follows immediately upon baptism, the postbaptismal anointing, as well as the formula which accompanies it, are suppressed.

This rubric contains important theological substance: Would this mean that in this case it is confirmation which confers the gift of the priesthood of the faithful?

It seems strange that this gift can be attributed at one time to baptism, and at another to confirmation. Does this not take away from the distinctiveness of the different sacraments? The problem can thus be laid at the door of the *Ordo* of baptism itself. On the other hand, we now have an *Ordo* which not only refers to the priesthood of the faithful, but even specifies the particular act which confers it. . . .

The questions facing theologians are therefore:

1) Can one speak of a sacrament which confers priest-hood upon the faithful? Do the *Praenotanda* of the *Ordo initiationis* really authorize us to do so?

2) How can we understand the *Ordo* which attributes this conferring of the priesthood sometimes to baptism, and at other times implicitly to confirmation?

3) If this gift is indeed part of confirmation, should we not then expand on what we normally say about confirmation, that it gives strength and the grace to bear witness, and say that it gives the strength to proclaim the kingdom and also to actuate sacramentally what is proclaimed: In other words, that confirmation therefore confers priesthood?

The theology of confirmation therefore needs to be enriched; this is indicated by the *Ordo* of baptism in the rubric for the post-baptismal anointing, a rubric which contains a contradiction in what is taught in the *Praenotanda,* which designates the postbaptismal anointing with chrism as the gift of priesthood, a gift which cannot be omitted, even if there is no anointing, when confirmation follows immediately upon baptism. So it would be in this case confirmation which takes over the conferring of this gift of priesthood. . . .

But what has been brought out here is very important. If what we have written is true, it would be impossible habitually to confer the Eucharist upon persons who have not yet been confirmed. This would be possible only if one had only a partial vision of the reality of the Eucharist: The real presence of Christ. As soon as one sees the Eucharist as the celebration and the offering of the sacrifice of Christ with him present, it is hard to see how someone who has not yet been called to this role of priestly offering can be directly associated in it.

It seems that we are here once again in a position to ask the theologians for an explanation which, moreover, would be of great import for pastoral teaching and for the catechesis of the sacrament of confirmation.

3) The pastoral teaching of confirmation

Can there be a pastoral teaching of confirmation that has no basis in tradition or theology? We must be able to put ourselves in the shoes of a bishop or priest, charged with the pastoral care of the youngest Christians of today, and feel their anguish. They are more heavily burdened today than in the past. The statistics are troublesome, in certain countries in particular, when we compare the number of the baptized with the number of the practicing. Today the question seems to rise spontaneously as to whether we do not need either a specific sacrament or at least some very strong intervention on the part of the Church at the moment when a young Christian reaches maturity, which might help him or her remain a practicing Christian.

Such a suggestion is certainly justified, yet before we look into it further should we not pause a moment to consider the undeniable absence in the Church of today of any well-organized mystagogy? The consequences of such a lack are readily observed.

The custom today is to confer confirmation at twelve years of age, which means we think that young people of this age are capable of assuming the concomitant responsibilites. But when confirmation is conferred along with what is—strangely—called "Solemn Communion," the young Christian is thereafter abandoned to his or her own devices, unless, of course, they happen to attend a Christian school. Even though a certain number of groups of all kinds have been created, there exists nowhere any obligatory mystagogy, such as we find in antiquity. The young Christian has no on-going framework of education, and no community of Christians is there to help him or her, and in this way supplement or, if need be, replace the support of the family which may be deficient. There is a large choice of Christian groups available to the young Christian, but none are obligatory, and they do not follow naturally upon the young person's previous Christian education; they also lack a truly personalized support system.

The same may be said of the sacrament of marriage. The newlyweds have no support from a warm Christian community which could help them along their path to Christ. It may well be that the parish as support system will have to be replaced progressively by some sort of "community"—but here we are getting into yet another problem.

It appears that we need to take another look at how we view the nature of a sacrament. It is not a magical action which so transforms the one who receives it that he or she needs no further help from the community in order to progress in the gift which was conferred in the sacrament. It is for this reason that putting off confirmation until age twelve, as we have done, or the suggested age of eighteen, would be no help at all. We might even question waiting for a child to be seven years old before conferring the Eucharist. The reason was that we expected those years to prepare him or her, but in fact, have they? A sacrament is not an act of magic: it requires a strong and personalized support system.

The statistics, which are cruel, should make us realize that what is needed is above all a mystagogy, rather than a sacrament. The usual reaction to these awful statistics is to want to spread out the conferring of the sacraments over even more years, with confirmation put off until age eighteen (when the person is supposedly more mature), in order to keep in touch, as it were, with the child, who otherwise would have little contact with the Church. Whereas, in antiquity, and in Rome at least until the twelfth century, all the sacraments were conferred at once upon the infant.

Is this line of reasoning legitimate, or is there a trace of unconscious Pelagianism in such a projection? To be sure, the goal is a spiritual maturity that everyone strongly desires. But in order to arrive at this goal, our anxieties lead us to refuse the gift of the Spirit, conferring wisdom and strength, to the young person in need of maturing into Christian adulthood, as if these gifts of the Spirit were some sort of reward for having attained maturity, instead of being a means to that very end. It is curious to note that in the West, where a theology of the character of the sacraments is highly developed, it seems scarcely drawn on pastorally. An example is the sacrament of confirmation, which, if it is conferred at a very young age, continues to bring its gifts to bear as they are needed. It is as if we were more attached to celebrating the sacrament at the point in time when we feel its need. If this should prove to be the case for the Eucharist, which does not confer a sacramental character, is it also true for confirmation, which does confer a character, and cannot be repeated as can the Eucharist?

This lack in the Western Church of a developed theology of the gifts of the Spirit, at least on the subject of confirmation, is truly astonishing, as is the reliance on the personal and private efforts of the individual in acquiring spiritual maturity, while also forgetting that it is, of course, the Spirit which is the surest guarantor of such maturation.

But what is perhaps the most astonishing of all is that our pastoral procedures draw very little on either tradition or theology. As regards confirmation, our concern here, the most rudimentary study of tradition will show that present-day pastoral practice is not in conformity at all with what has gone before. From a theological point of view, as we have seen above, conferring the Eucharist before confirmation lies, as a practice, outside of the theology of the sacrament. For pastoral reasons, we have ignored the inherent reality of the sacrament. It is our position that we need this sacrament in order to develop an adult attitude towards our Christianity.

We therefore ask those with pastoral responsibilites to come offer their opinion on a very important question: Should the structure and the contents of a sacrament give way to pastoral needs, or should pastoral practice be based on the sacrament? Put differently, can a pastoral decision spring from a pastoral need, ignoring all other considerations?

No one would suggest that the Church has the right to put more meaning into a sacrament than was meant by Christ. This holds true of the very establishment of the sacrament, its structure, its form, and its make-up. But does this mean that we can ignore important traditional contributions? This holds true as well for the discipline of a sacrament. The opinion of pastors would be welcomed here. Is it their belief that we can today, for the sacrament of confirmation, let the Church ignore its basic character and tolerate a contradiction in her teachings, which, on the one hand, speak of the priesthood of the baptized, and then of the confirmed, while she allows the conferring of the Eucharist upon those who have not yet been prepared through confirmation to receive it?

Does it not seem that this should only be allowed in emergency situations, when all other means have been exhausted? And to say that today is today, and the past is the past, is truly a frivolous attitude.

4) Renunciation, profession of faith, and confirmation

As we study these considerations, it seems necessary to make a distinction between renunciation, profession of faith, and confirmation. If this last should not be unduly put off, which would deprive the Christian of strength, there is no reason not to put off the act of renunciation and the profession of faith, which could be made solemnly and publicly at a more mature age. If one believes in the permanent character conferred by confirmation, there is no reason to wait until the young Christian makes his or her renunciation and profession of faith.

Now, in our modern *Ordo* these last two acts are rightly associated with confirmation, in order to affirm in a concrete way what was done at baptism, when the child had no understanding. Renunciation and the profession of faith are necessary before receiving the sacraments of Christian initiation. These fundamental acts are always required of an adult. However, from earliest times the Church has baptized, confirmed, and given the Eucharist to infants with no understanding, relying on the faith of their parents and of the Church, feeling that the child should be brought into the side of the Good, and assuming responsibility for their education and their eventual personal ratification of this renunciation and this profession of faith.

It appears that it is at this point that the first question arises: Is it possible that baptism is too readily conferred upon children who have no one truly responsible for their initiation? Of course, we do not want to turn down candidates for baptism if it can be avoided, even though this is sometimes necessary. But would it not be possible to imagine a sort of catechumenate such as was familiar to *Roman Ordo XI,* contemporaneous with the *Gelasian Sacramentary*? Such a catechumenate would involve the parents in the successive exorcisms of their child, and they would therefore be catechized themselves for their child's baptism. Such a requirement for the baptism of a child would pave the way for a solid Christian education for him or her, and would ensure support in formative years later on, when the young person will hypothetically be confirmed and will receive Communion for the first time. At this point the child will have pronounced his or her renunciation and made the appropriate promises. In a supportive Christian environment, he or she will reach adult age, eighteen or twenty years, at which time the Church would require a solemnized act of renunciation and the profession of faith.

These proposals require some elaboration. At this point, we suggest the following: Inasmuch as we practice the baptism of children, we could then confer confirmation (before conferring the Eucharist) at around seven years of age, since the parents will have received a catechesis, especially if they are not fully believers, or at least because the child has responsible sponsors to guide him or her. As the chid matures with guidance, he or she will then be ready to make the act of solemn renunciation and profession of faith towards the age of eighteen or twenty years.

5) A DEMANDING MYSTAGOGY WHICH LEADS TO A DECISIVE ACT OF PERSONAL COMMITMENT

We have noted above the conditions which we propose for conferring baptism on a child. After confirmation and First Holy Communion at age seven, the child's formation must continue as a long mystagogy until age eighteen or twenty.

Now how, concretely, can this be accomplished? First, if the parents themselves have been prepared for the baptism of their child, they will be more disposed to have the child receive the mystagogy that the Church offers him or her. But the child is more likely to continue his or her instruction if having done so is a requirement for being allowed, at age eighteen or twenty, to make the solemn pronounciation of the baptismal promises and the profession of faith. The young person could also be refused if his or her public behavior were less than desirable. And if he or she is not allowed to make this public profession of faith, then the sacraments would also be denied until such time as the Church finds the young person meets requirements.

All this, of course, represents quite an innovation, absent up until now in the modern Church. Some may be quite taken aback by these suggestions, but it is the position of the writer that, with things as they are today, without some "new" degree of severity the Church may find herself more and more lacking in credibility.

What we are proposing represents, in fact, a double vigilance towards those who are about to commit themselves to the Church. First, we are strict about admitting them to the sacrament of baptism: We require that the parents be responsible for the education of the child, or else they must come up with someone who will be, in their place. Baptism could, however, be allowed on the condition that the parents accept a long catechesis for themselves which will provide them with a genuine Christian education, and if they accept the obligations incumbent upon them as their child's sponsors for his or her upbringing in the Faith. This responsibility includes making sure that their child receives instruction until the age of about seven, when he or she will make a first solemn act of renunciation, pronounce solemnly his or her baptismal promises with full consciousness this time, and then receive confirmation and First Holy Communion. After this the child will receive a mystagogy which will lead up to the act of renunciation and the promises made, at this time, at a more mature age.

6) How shall this mystagogy be set up for the child from age seven to about eighteen or twenty?

Clearly it would not be appropriate to legislate in the abstract. Each episcopal Conference must make its own arrangements as seems best locally.

The catechesis should not consist only of classes, but should also include liturgical celebrations in support of what is taught, along the lines of *Roman Ordo XI* as cited above. Another possible source would lie in adapting what is provided for catechumens in preparation for their Christian initiation. This is not the place to attempt a detailed proposal for this catechesis. Let it suffice to refer the reader to the catechumenate of adults, which could be adapted without too much trouble.

In fact, what we are proposing lies half-way between the organization of the so-called "neo-catechumenate" groups, and a destructive laxism, or even the total absence of any mystagogy.

What appears evident is that we must get used to the idea of a certain degree of severity without compromise, even though we realize that this may well lead to the loss of future Christians. Perhaps we should admit that they are already lost. We are not suggesting the creation of a religion for the elite: Throwing out of the net those fish of lesser quality. But we must be sure that we have an authentic Church. Sinners belong to such a Church, but on the condition that they acknowledge that they are sinners and make efforts toward their conversion: We cannot accept those who want an exteriorized religion without any real inner commitment.

Some may find it too severe to deny the sacraments to those who cannot, or do not care to, pronounce the public renunciation and baptismal promises. Yet how can we bring to the sacraments someone who does not intend to confess publicly his or her faith?

Obviously, there is a lot of work to be done, and we need a great deal of patience and prudence. But it is our firm belief that if we allow a young Christian to receive the gift of the Spirit in a supportive, structured environment, he or she will mature to the point of being able to make public proclamation of the Faith. The gift of the Spirit will not be a future reward for earlier efforts on the part of the young person, but it is the Spirit who will have brought him or her to this decisive moment. The strength conferred in confirmation, and the exercising of the priesthood received in confirmation and acting in the Eucharist, will together bear their fruit.

So it is not flying in the face of tradition or the theology of the sacrament of confirmation that we can ensure the growth of the Church, but by giving it some deep thought, and by creating a structured environment that will be able to reinforce the identity of the person who commits him or herself to a true encounter with Christ, in his Church.

b) A perusal of the liturgy

1) THE REASON FOR THE NEW RITUAL OF 1971

The *Ordo* that we were working with had its merits. For one, it was clear. The rites and the texts expressed clearly what was meant. It did, however, contain some weaknesses, and it should be of use to amend them.

a) The sacrament of confirmation is, in our day, in most cases, separated from baptism and the Eucharist. Moreover, the rite itself is very brief: the imposition of the hands and anointing. Early on some amplification was seen as desirable.

The *Romano-Germanic Pontifical* of the tenth century found it indispensable to bring in certain elements, both before and after the rite of confirmation itself, that were intended to make the ritual more solid, to the thinking of those who were working in Mayence on Roman custom.[30*] These additions were repeated in the *Roman Pontifical* of the twelfth century[31*], and by the *Roman Pontifical* of the thirteenth century.[32*] The *Pontifical of Guillaume Durand* of the end of the thirteenth century also repeats these additions, but it provides also for the celebration of confirmation by itself.[33*] This example will be followed in all subsequent rituals, by that of Paul V and its following editions under other Pontiffs down to Vatican II.

These excrescences introduced into these rituals diminished the importance of the essential elements of the sacrament. The new post-Vatican II ritual has remedied this situation in an admirable way. It placed the ritual of confirmation after the homily of the Mass and before the offertory. If confirmation is not celebrated during Mass, a Liturgy of the Word is provided to introduce it.

b) We must take note of the fact that the new *Ordo* clearly wants the sacrament of confirmation to be preceded by the baptismal renunciation and promises, underscoring in this way the connection between the two sacraments. This may be somewhat artificial, since the majority of those about to be confirmed have already received the Eucharist, but still the underlying relationship between baptism and confirmation is emphasized.

c) In the ancient *Ordo,* the anointing was accompanied by a prayer describing what was happening: "Confirmo te chrismate salutis. . . ." But the purpose of the anointing was not mentioned. Our new *Ordo* chose a new prayer, of Byzantine origin and with no precedent in Latin tradition, which expresses the purpose of the sacrament: "Accipe donum Spiritus Sancti" ("receive the gift of the Spirit"). To be precise, the prayer has: "Accipe signaculum doni Spiritus Sancti" ("receive the seal of the gift of the Spirit"): A somewhat ambiguous expression, because it is not the sign which one receives, but the gift of the Spirit, expressed by the sign.

d) After the anointing, the old ritual prescribed a light blow on the cheek of the confirmand, given by the bishop. This practice is found at the end of the thirteenth century in the *Pontifical of Guillaume Durand.* It seems highly probable that this gesture has something to do with the ritual for the investiture of knights, in keeping with a theology of confirmation stressing its character of bearing witness. The new *Ordo* fortunately has suppressed this practice and replaced it with what is suggested in the beginning of the third century in the *Apostolic Tradition* of Hippolytus of Rome: The kiss of peace, given by the bishop to the confirmand, who is from now on fully committed to the Church, and who can now participate in the prayers of the faithful and, for the first time, in the Eucharist.

The above was intended to bring to mind certain merits of

the old ritual and the new, which will color the individual critiques which follow.

2) CAN THE IMMUTABILITY OF THE APOSTOLIC CONSTITUTION *Divinae consortium naturae* BE QUESTIONED?

The ritual of 1971 is introduced by an Apostolic Constitution signed by Pope Paul VI, normal practice in such cases as this, when the *Ordo* has been rather radically altered.

Before proceeding to a critique of the *Ordo,* we might be permitted the luxury of a look at the bearing this Constituion has on faith, and on discipline as well. Is it meant to be immutable?

The end of the text of the Apostolic Constitution seems to give a very good answer to our question:

> This is why, in order that the rite of confirmation correspond perfectly to the very essence of the sacramental rite, with our Supreme Apostolic Authority we decree and we establish that what follows be in the future observed in the Latin Church: The sacrament of confirmation is conferred "by the anointing with chrism on the forehead," which takes place "by the imposition of the hand," as well as by the words: "Receive the seal of the gift of the Holy Spirit."[34]*

This passage beginning "qua propter" ("this is why") is the conclusion of the entire Constitution. What remains to be done, according to the right and the duty of the Church, is to determine clearly what are the essential conditions for a valid sacrament: ". . . ad ipsam etiam ritus sacramentalis essentiam congruenter pertineat" ("so that the rite of confirmation correspond perfectly to the very essence of the sacrmental rite"). It is on these conditions for validity that the supreme Authority exercises its power: ". . . decernimus et constituimus" ("we decree and establish"). Nevertheless, this discipline only concerns the *Ecclesia latina.* There are, therefore, Eastern Churches in communion with Rome which consider that the one essential rite is the imposition, and not the anointing—and this, either from the very beginning, or under the influence of the Roman Church. So these Churches are not affected by these dispositons for the validity of the sacrament. The word *servantur* is crucial: What we have here is discipline, a grave discipline undoubtedly, since it concerns the validity of the sacrament, but we cannot mistake this discipline for a propositon of faith—this discipline must be "observed." So we have here a disciplinary Constitution, setting down the required elements for a valid sacrament, but not making them a matter of faith, even if one must believe that only this way of celebrating the sacrament gives it its validity. The expression *in posterum* clearly does not mean "forever," but now, for the future, until directives to the contrary.

It is therefore forbidden for anyone not to observe these directives as a whole or in part, since they concern the validity of the sacrament. But it remains legitimate to study them and to make respectful suggestions for modifications, even substantial ones.[35]*

Unfortunately, the phrase which describes the essential gestures is quite obscure. For one thing, it is clearly indicated that the sacrament of confirmation will henceforth be conferred by anointing. This changes startingly the connection between the sacrament and Scripture, in which the Spirit, especially in Acts, is given by the imposition of hands. It also represents a rupture with Latin tradition, which has always made the imposition of hands or of the hand part of the valid sacrament. However, the way in which this anointing is done implies the impositon of the hand (singular). The anointing is done by the imposition of the hand. This is scarcely comprehensible and cannot be interpreted as the meaning of what Benedict XIV prescribed: Imposition on the head of the right hand, while the bishop confers the anointing with his thumb. This interpretation was rejected by the Congregation itself. Are we to understand, bizarrely, that the signing with the thumb is considered to be the imposition of the hand? It must be admitted that the most important phrase of the Constitution is really obscure; one might even be tempted to see in it an unfortunate interpretation of the letter of Innocent III, explaining that what is conferred in the Eastern Churches by anointing is conferred, among the Latins, by the imposition of the hand. But clearly that is not what the Constitution means.

3) THE IMPOSITION OF THE HAND, OR OF THE HANDS? ON ALL THE CONFIRMANDS AT ONCE? ON EACH ONE SEPARATELY?

The text of the Constitution uses the singular *manus impositione* (imposition of the hand), referring to ancient sources. We should note that the Constitution itself, despite its concrete directives, declares—using this time the plural *manuum* (hands)—"Quae manuum impositio ex traditione catholica merito agnoscitur initium sacramenti confirmationis" ("This imposition of the hands, according to Catholic tradition is, justifiably, considered the beginning of the sacrment of confirmation"). It goes on to enumerate in the notes a considerable number of liturgical documents that deal with the imposition of the hand and with the sign of the cross. It is surely legitimate to be surprised that, after such painstaking research into the documentation and after reaching such correct conclusions, the Constitution should have made decisions so contradictory to the most ancient tradition. It might be more easily understood if the Constitution had done so in order to make the rite better understood, or to provide a clearer catechesis. But, on the contrary, the catechist will not find in Acts that the gift of the Spirit is given by anointing, but by the imposition of the hands. He will therefore be in difficulties if he takes Scripture as his point of departure for a catechesis of the sacrament, and just as much so if he wishes to start from the ritual, as ought to be the norm. And this ritual, let us emphasize once again, has the bishop impose his hands with a prayer that asks the Father to send his Spirit, but which hastens to say that neither the gesture nor the text actualize at this point what they signify only in appearance, since the Spirit is given in the anointing which follows. In other words, these acts are without efficacity.

But perhaps we should better look at the question of the singular or plural—hand, or hands?

Let us take a look, then, in our principal sources where there is mention of the imposition of the hand (singular) upon everyone at the same time, and upon each one individually; and then imposition of the hands (plural), both upon all at once, and upon the individual.

The *Apostolic Tradition* of Hippolytus speaks of the imposition of the hand (singular) upon all at the same time.[36*] The same practice is found in the *Gelasian Sacramentary*,[37*] the *Gellone Sacramentary*,[38*] and the *Romano-Germanic Pontifical* of the Tenth Century: Imposition of the hand (singular) upon all the confirmands *at the same time*. The *Roman Pontifical* of the Twelfth Century[40*] and the one of the *Roman Curia* in the Thirteenth Century[41*] contain a different rubric: ". . . "imposita manu super capita singulorum" ("imposition of the hand [singular] on each one").

At the end of the thirteenth century, the *Pontifical of Guillaume Durand*[42]* is alone in offering the following rubric: "... elevatis et super confirmandos extensis manibus, dicit" ("... with his hands raised and stretched out over the confirmands, he says ..."). In this case we have the imposition of the hands (plural) over all at the same time.

Therefore, from the beginning of the third century until the beginning of the thirteenth, we find the imposition of the hand (singular). It is done, however, in two different ways: Over all the confirmands at the same time, from the beginning of the third century until the tenth-eleventh centuries; and on each one of the confirmands, in the twelfth and the beginning of the thirteenth centuries. The imposition of the hands (plural) upon all the confirmands together is found at the end of the thirteenth century. This last directive will be repeated in the ritual of Paul V and all of its later editions under different Pontiffs, until Vatican II.

Do these differences correspond to particular theological distinctions? We should note that the imposition of the hand (singular) upon all the confirmands at the same time is the most frequently mentioned, and that the imposition of the hands (plural) over all is the latest in time. In any case, we see that the presence of this imposition separated from the anointing is noted in all the sources, even when the anointing assumes greater importance in the *Ordo*. The Roman Pontificals of the twelfth and thirteenth centuries stand out from among all the others in having the imposition of the hand upon each confirmand individually. One cannot help wanting to know with certitude whether or not there is a theological reason behind this difference. We are given no explanation. One more or less plausible hypothesis is the following: These Pontificals might have been reacting to a certain diminishing of the importance of the imposition of the hand, in favor of anointing, which would have been more compatible with a theology of matter (oil) and form (*Confirmo te chrismate*), concerned with preserving the importance of the imposition of the hand in the administration of the sacrament and in keeping with scriptural and liturgical tradition. Individual imposition certainly emphasizes the gesture; as for the anointing, each confirmand was very clearly the object of the imposition of the hand. But this is only hypothetical.

The Apostolic Constitution *Divinae consortium naturae,* in

that unfortunately obscure passage on the way in which the sacrament is to be conferred, uses the singular: The anointing is done by the imposition of the hand.

No one can deny the sybilline character of this phrase. This being so, and above all because we are dealing with a discipline concerning the validity of a sacrament, we might ask ourselves if it would not be a good idea to study the matter again and to express it in clear language. The Constitution on the Liturgy demands that the rites be easily understood.[43*] Faced with an undeniable obscurity, it is equally undeniable that something must be done about it.

4) POSTBAPTISMAL ANOINTING AND THE ANOINTING OF CONFIRMATION

The problem of the postbaptismal anointing, in our new rituals, is closely bound to confirmation. What is astonishing—and on this point we must pause a moment and look at it from a liturgical point of view—is the rubric which provides that this anointing and the accompanying prayer be omitted if confirmation is to follow. We have already discussed the theological problem caused by this rubric (is the priesthood of the faithful conferred in baptism or in confirmation?[44*]) This rubric which suppresses the anointing when confirmation follows seems to transfer the gift of the priesthood to confirmation.

But what interests us here is the reason behind this suppression of the postbaptismal anointing and its accompanying prayer, when confirmation follows immediately. The impression given is that this suppression simply wishes to avoid duplication: One anointing after baptism with chrism, done by the priest, and then, a short time afterwards, another anointing with chrism, conferred this time by the bishop. Ignoring hoary tradition, one of the two anointings was seen as superfluous, and it was the one after baptism that had to be sacrificed. In this way, the importance of the anointing of confirmation was increased. Here again, deeper theological work and some fine tuning need to be done, followed by adjustments in the rites themselves. As they are now, our rites remain very vague. On the one hand, they have increased the importance of the postbaptismal anointing by changing its accompanying prayer, as well as by attributing to baptism the gift of the Spirit or by stating that it is baptism that confers this gift.

On the other hand, when confirmation follows, this anointing is suppressed altogether. How can we let such inconsistency stand, regardless of the fact that it was not noticed at the time it was composed?

5) A TEXT AND A GESTURE THAT LACK AUTHENTICITY

Despite its obvious intent to emphasize the ritual of anointing, the new *Ordo* of confirmation has kept the gesture of the impositon of the hands upon all the confirmands at the same time, following the *Pontifical of Guillaume Durand,* as we saw above, accompanied by the ancient Gelasian prayer asking the Father to send the Spirit. The enumeration of the seven gifts follows.

The Constitution *Divinae consortium naturae* conceals neither scriptural traditon nor our old liturgical traditon. It does, however, seem to have apparently been guided by the position of "many doctors in sacred theology who have thought that the validity of confirmation resides solely in the anointing done by the imposition of the hand on the forehead(?)." The text, however, goes on to say that "in the Latin Church the imposition of the hands before the anointing with chrism was always prescribed." Now, if we ask just who were these doctors in holy theology, we see that they can easily be found together at one point in time, sharing the same mentality and the desire to apply the theology of matter and form to the sacraments.

It is hard not to feel that the commission which prepared the new ritual let itself be seduced by this tendency, ignoring centuries of tradition and the undeniable origin of the rite in the New Testament. This rejection of all biblical and liturgical tradition is astonishing, given the diametrically opposed position of the theologians of Pius XII for the study of the ordinations. These theologians, based on their study of tradition, were able to show that the imposition of the hands alone was essential for ordination, and that the other rites, such as the anointing of the hands, etc., were subsidiary. Even granted that the documentation is undoubtedly less abundant for the history of confirmation, a simple glance through the sacramentaries and the pontificals should be enough, one would think, to support the same conclusions as for the ordinations.

The "doctors of sacred theology" referred to in the Apostolic Constitution do not appear to have attributed to the imposition of the hands the validity of the sacrament, which, according to them, resides solely in the anointing. But they do, however, leave the imposition in, even though it and its accompanying prayer are reduced to the function of vestigial organs, purely ceremonial and without authenticity. The most one could grant them would be to say, as does our present ritual, that they have the value of preparatory rites to the receiving of the sacrament in the anointing.

But if in the tenth and even still in the thirteenth centuries such gestures and words without authenticity—mere ceremonial evocations—did not shock anyone, the same is not true today.

The Constitution on the Liturgy is very clear about this: ". . . verba sancta, quae significant clarius exprimant, eaque populus christianus, in quantum fieri potest facile percipere . . . possit" ("the holy words must express more clearly what they mean and the Christian people, as much as possible, must be able easily to understand them"). The Constitution *Divinae consortium naturae* repeats this text for the case of confirmation.

As it stands, the enactment of the ritual is in flagrant contradiction with this wish, to such an extent that one could say with no exaggeration that the unaware faithful could truly be led into error by the rites and the words.

For the bishop gives a little speech in which he says that the baptized who are before him are going to receive the Spirit, and for this he asks the prayer of all. After a moment of impressive silence, the bishop imposes his hands upon all the confirmands at the same time, and, using the old Gelasian formula, asks the Father to send upon these baptized perons his Spirit of strength, wisdom, etc.

How are we not to believe that at this moment the Spirit is poured out upon these baptized? How are we not to believe that there is a reality which corresponds to this gesture and these words? But rubric no. 29 declares that this imposition of the hands does not confer the Spirit. . . . Nothing could be more opposed to the mentality of liturgical renewal than such a lack of authenticity. And how are we to understand, a few lines after the rubric which denies the whole meaning of the gesture and the words pronounced by the bishop, this explanation which cannot, unfortunately, be applied here: "Per impositionem manuum super confirmandos ab Episcopo ac sacerdotibus concelebrantibus factam, biblicus gestus exprimitur, quo Spiritus Sancti donum invocatur, modo optime aptato intelligentiae populi christiani. . . ." ("By the imposition of the hands of the Bishop and the concelebrating priests upon the confirmands the biblical gesture is expressed, through which the Holy Spirit is invoked in an excellent manner, adapted to the understanding of the Christian people. . . .")? Do the Christian people in fact understand clearly what is going on? Or are they, on the contrary, deceived? For even if the rubric says so, the Christian people present do not know that there is no reality corresponding to the biblical gesture and the words, and that these have no effect. So the gesture and the words are misunderstood, and the catechist is hard put to find a way to explain the liturgy of the sacrament. If he should take as his point of departure, as one ought to, the ritual itself, he will have to say that the gesture of the imposition of the hands and the words that accompany it are not efficacious, because they do not mean what they ought to mean. . . . But if he takes Scripture as his point of departure, he will not find an anointing as the sign of the gift of the Spirit, but rather the imposition of the hands; the Constitution itself says it clearly: The imposition of the hands was the beginning of the sacrament of confirmation.

We may therefore legitimately claim that for two reasons—simplicity and clarity—the ritual must be made over, to get rid of too many important contradictions and its ambiguity in regard to the stated wishes of the Constitution on the Liturgy. The present ritual is the result of a method of working that prefers a theological concept to scriptural texts and the most ancient tradition. The theology of the matter and the form of the sacrament wins over Scripture. The preferred "matter" in this case is the anointing, supplanting the imposition of the hands, although this last was deemed of pastoral value even though it did not correspond to any theological system. So it seems that we canonot avoid redoing the ritual. Simply editing it as it stands would not be possible; we cannot knowingly keep on walking down the wrong path.

6) A few suggestions

1. Now that each of the rituals of Christian initiation has been studied anew, they could be brought together into one volume, under the title of *Christian Initiation*. This book would contain the following sections (after the rewritten *Praenotanda*): (1) the ritual for Christian initiation for adults; (2) the ritual for Chris-

tian initiation for children; (3) the ritual for confirmation; (4) the Eucharist as the culminating point of Christian initition.

2. In the ritual of baptism, at the end of the celebration and during the postbaptismal anointing, the text of the Gelasian formula would be used, leaving out "Ut eius aggregatur populo Christi sacerdotis, prophetae et regis. . . ."; The anointing therefore would be practiced, as it was from earliest times right down to Vatican II, even if confirmation follows immediately. It could be considered as the sigillum and the illustration of baptism, just as one could consider the anointing of confirmation as the sigillum of the gift of the Spirit conferred by the imposition of the hands.

3. In the *Praenotanda,* at III *De sacramenti celebratione,* the following changes would be introduced: "The sacrament of confirmation is conferred by the imposition of the hand or the hands and by the anointing on the forehead with the words: "Receive the seal of the gift of the Holy Spirit."[45]*

The two paragraphs: "As for the impositon of the hands . . . the priests who assist the main celebrant . . ." would be suppressed and replaced by:

> The bishop alone imposes his hand (or hands) upon the confirmands. If they are not too numerous, the bishop imposes his hand upon each one individually. He can do this in two different ways: Either he says over each one the prayer "Almighty God . . .," or else he says this prayer while imposing his hand over everyone at once, and then imposes his hand upon each one individually, but in silence. If the confirmands are numerous, the bishop says the prayer while imposing his hands over all of them at one time.

The entire rite has a double meaning: The imposition of the hand or hands by the bishop upon the confirmands expresses the biblical gesture through which the Spirit is invoked, an excellent and easily understood gesture for the Christian people. In order for the authenticity of the text to be verified, when the bishop imposes his hand, the Spirit is poured out. In the anointing with chrism and in the words which accompany it the gift of the Holy Spirit is clearly meant.[46]*

4. At the beginning of the homily prepared for the bishop, it would be more exact to write, instead of "Apostoli qui, in die

Pentecostes" ("the Apostles, who on the day of Pentecost"), rather: "Apostoli, qui cum discipulis suis, die Pentecostes . . ." ("the Apostles, who, with the disciples, on the day of Pentecost. . . .").

5. At number 25 the rubric should be changed as follows: "Next the bishop alone imposes his hand or hands upon all the confirmands, saying. . . ."[47*]

After the text of the prayer, these new rubrics could be inserted:

> The bishop can confirm in two different ways, if the confirmands are not too numerous, or if he judges it opportune: Standing, he imposes his hands upon all the confirmands, saying. . . . Next the bishop sits down and imposes his hand on each one, in silence. Or alternatively, the bishop is seated and imposes his hand on each one saying over each the prayer "Almighty God. . . ."[48*]

7) EXPLANATION AND JUSTIFICATION OF THESE SUGGESTIONS

1. The impositon of the hands and of the hand rightfully regains its original importance by drawing on ancient and continuous tradition as well as the biblical sources. Imposition would be indispensable for the validity of the sacrament of confirmation and would not be confused with the anointing. In this way the gesture would be authentic, and the ancient prayer which accompanies it would be given back its proper importance.

Two different ways, both in conformity with tradition, are suggested here. One of the two could be selected, or both could be allowed to remain, to provide a choice at the discretion of the bishop.

The bishop would extend his hand (singular) upon all of the confirmands at the same time, saying the *Gelasian* prayer provided in the ritual. Or else he could impose his hand on each one of the confirmands, repeating the prayer each time. This is only possible in the case of few confirmands, but it is attested as well in the twelfth-thirteenth centuries.

We offer yet a third suggestion, a non-traditional one: The bishop imposes both hands over all at the same time, while saying the prayer, and then he imposes his hand upon each one individually in silence.

The objection may possibly be raised that giving the imposition of the hands such importance could confuse this rite with that of the ordination of a priest. The answer is easy: The imposition of the hands has the efficacity that the words designate. Hands are imposed variously at the ordination of a bishop, a priest, or a deacon, and there is no confusion as to which order is being conferred. Now that the theology of the priesthood of the faithful has been clarified, this imposition of the hands at confirmation is very meaningful and leads to no possible confusion.

2. Even if it is considered necessary for the validity of the sacrament, the anointing could be conferred by the priests who are there with the bishop, as our present *Ordo* provides.

D. The Eucharist as Crowning Experience of Christian Initiation

There is no doubt whatsoever that the Eucharist is, according to tradition and even theology, the crowning experience of Christian initiation. Every initiation has as its purpose to form a new person, a person of the Covenant, member of a new people and a new race, called as priests to proclaim and bring about, in conjunction with the ordained priesthood and in union with Christ, the unique High Priest, the sacrificial activity of reconciliation and of praise of the Father. The institution of the Eucharist has as its primary purpose the existence of a sacrament which actualizes in the present the sacrifice of reconciliation and of praise, so that all the baptized may become actors in this reconstruction of the Covenant.

It is possible that theological thought may have at times downgraded to second place what is actually the essence of the sacrament. It is typical to see so many manuals which treat of the Eucharist consecrate pages and pages to its character as real presence and as sacrament, but spend little ink on its nature as sacrifice. It is also possible that the very legitimate and meaningful adoration of the host has led at least some of us to lose sight of the Eucharist's being first and foremost the active offering of sacrifice. Christian initiation is therefore entirely oriented toward this grace conferred upon the initiate to enable him or her, along with Christ and in conjunction with the ordained priest who alone can enact it, to offer the unique sacrifice of Christ, present before him or her.

With this in mind, the practice of inverting the two sacraments and conferring the Eucharist before confirmation, apparently for pastoral reasons, appears all the more astonishing.

The restoration of the ritual for adults has done nothing to highlight the importance of this first Eucharistic celebration of the initiate. It would perhaps have been a good idea to do so. It may be that when the work was being done those involved were either not sensitive to, or feared pointing out, the serious anomaly which consists in giving the sign of the culmination of initiation to someone who is not yet completely initiated. For this is what happens each time we give Communion to someone who will be confirmed afterwards.

There are a number of possible ways in which to emphasize the exceptional experience of this Eucharistic celebration for the initiate. For instance, it could be done with a specific address at the moment when the initiate brings the bread and wine for the sacrifice up to the altar. (And at this juncture let us stress one more time the grave anomaly that consists in giving the Eucharist to the initiate with bread consecrated at a prior Mass. This is truly the worst case of being insensitive to the quality of the sign, a situation which we find, alas, all too often the case.)

At the very moment of Communion there could be an appropriate short address, such as: "Blessed are you to be invited for the first time to the Supper of the Lord, with all our community" (or something similar).

We might wonder whether the practice cited in the *Apostolic Tradition* could not be used. By giving to the initiate as well as to all the faithful a catechesis explaining the symbolism of the water offered to the initiate, and of the milk and the honey, it seems that this would not constitute an archeological return to the past, but a valid emphasizing of the meaning of this first participation in the Eucharist.

It seems that at this point a particular remark needs to be made: For after these somewhat uncommon celebrations, such as the renunciation, the anointing before and after baptism, the imposition of the hands, and the anointing of confirmation, the assembled faithful then find themselves again in familiar territory, a rite that they know well—the Eucharist. And they may not necessarily sense the particular richness of meaning of this Eucharist, the crowning experience of initiation.

Notes

¹* In his edition of the *Apostolic Tradition,* B. Botte emphasizes that we must not see in the liturgy presented in this book the accepted liturgy at Rome. He also clearly seems to attribute the work to Hippolytus. More recently, M. Mezger has offered a new way to look at the book, which he sees more as a collection of diverse practices, rather than a book written as one work. He also casts some doubt on the attribution to Hippolytus (see also the two articles in E.O.) In the *Apostolic Tradition,* nn. 15-20 for the entry into and the organization of the catechumenate; n. 21 for the sacraments of initiation. Münster. The various editions have preserved the same numbering of notes.

²* L. C. Mohlberg, Rome. The various editions have preserved the same numbering of notes. For the catechumenate and the Mass of the scrutinies, see nn. 193-199; 225-228; 254-257. For the exorcisms and the various celebrations of the catechumenate, see nn. 283-328; 419-424. For the sacraments of initiation, see nn. 449-452.

³* Andrieu, Louvain, 1960. The various editions have kept the same pagination and numbers of notes. *Les Ordines romani du haut moyen âge* (The *Ordines romani* of the High Middle Ages), *Ordo XI,* vol. 2, pp. 417-447. Louvain, 1960. The various editions have kept the same pagination and numbering of notes.

⁴* Jean-Diacre, *Lettre à Senarius* (John the Deacon, Letter to Senarius), ed. A. Wilmart, *Analecta Reginensia 5 Studi e Testi, 59* (Città del Vaticano, 1933).

⁵* *Gelasian Sacramentary,* nn. 193-199; 225-228; 254-257.

⁶* Ibid., nn. 193-199.

⁷* This rubric is not found in the *Gelasian* at the place for the second Sunday because the Mass of Ember Days was celebrated the morning of the Saturday of the Ordinations, nn. 157-167.

⁸* J. Mallet and A. Thibaut, *Les manuscrits en écriture bénéventaine de la Bibliothèque capitulaire de Bénévent* (The Manuscripts in Beneventan script of the Library of the Capitulary of Benevent), ed. CNRS Vol. 1, mss 1-18, 59; 175, n. 36; 241, n. 46.

⁹* This situation was preserved in the Missal of Pius V (so-called) which repeats as the Gospel for the second Sunday in Lent the Gospel for the Saturday, i.e., the Transfiguration.

¹⁰* *Ordo XI. Les Ordines romani du haut moyen âge,* vol. 2, 428-441, nn. 45-74.

¹¹* The *Gelasian Sacramentary,* nn. 195, 284, 289, 311, 419, 443, where the rubric designates children (*infantes*) as the object of a ritual.

¹²* A. Nocent, "Problemi contemporanei dell'iniziazione cristiana," *Rivista liturgica 54,* 1967, 81-94.

[13]* "Non quod in aqua Spiritum Sanctum consequimur, sed in aqua, emundati sub angelo, spiritui Sancto preparemur" (Tertullian, *De baptismo* 6, 1, *CCL* 1, 282).

[14]* Session XXIII, c. 4, *DS* 1774: "Si quis dixerit per sacram ordinationem non dari Spiritum Sanctum. . . ."

[15]* "Domine, Deus, sicut fecisti illos dignos accipere remissionem peccatorum in saeculum venturum, fac eos dignos ut repleantur Spiritu Sancto, et mitte super eos gratiam tuam, ut tibi serviant secundum volutatem tuam, quoniam tibi gloria. . . ." (Hippolytus of Rome, *La Tradition Apostolique*, ed. B. Botte, Münster im W. Aschendorf, 1963 (LGF 39) 21, 52-53).

[16]* Idem, 3, 8-9.

[17]* Idem, 3, 8-9.

[18]* Idem, 4, 16-17.

[19]* Idem, 21, 54-55.

[20]* Thomas Aquinas, *Summa Theologica,* III Pars q 72, a.5 ad 2; a 6 ad 1; a 9, ad 3.

[21]* "Sed ad recipientes pertinet sacramentum baptismi, quia per ipsum homo accipit potestatem recipiendi alia sacramenta: unde baptismum dicitur esse ianua omnium sacramentorum. Ad idem ordinatur quodammodo confirmatio, id est ad cultum" (Thomas Aquinas, Idem, III Pars, q 63, a. 8).

[22]* ". . .dicendum quod per ordinem et confirmationem deputantur fideles Christi ad aliqua specialia officia quae pertinent ad officum principis" (Idem, III Pars, q 65, a. 3).

[23]* Ambrose of Milan, *De sacramentis,* III, 2, 8-10, Sch 25 bis, 96-98.

[24]* *Lumen Gentium* nn. 10-11.

[25]* "Omnes enim in Christo regeneratos crucis signum effecit reges, Sancti Spiritus unctio consacrat sacerdotes, ut praeter ipsam specialem nostri ministeri servitutem, universi spiritales et rationabiles christiani agnoscant se regii generis et sacerdotalis officii esse consortes . . . Quod omnibus Dei gratiam commune sit factum, religiosum tamen vobis atque laudabile est, de die provectionis nostrae quasi de proprio honorore gaudere; ut cum celebratur in toto ecclesiae corpore pontificis sacramentum, quod, effuso benedictionis unguento, copiosus quidem in superiora profluxit, sed non parce etiam in inferiora descendit" (Leo the Great, *Sermon 4. In anniversario consecrationis ipsius, CCL* 138, 18-17).

[26]* "Deus, Pater omnipotens, qui te regeneravit ex aqua et spiritu concessitque tibi peccata tua ipse te unguet in vitam aeternam" (Ambrose of Milan, *De sacramentis,* II, 24, Sch 25 bis, 88-89).

[27]* "Deus omnipotens, Pater Domnini Nostri Iesu Christi, qui te regeneravit ex aqua et Spiritu Sancto, qui dedisti eis remissionem peccatorum, ipse te linit chrisma (sic) salutis in Christo Iesu domino nostro in vitam aeternam," in *Liber sacramentorum romanae ecclesiae ordinis circuli (Sacramentarium gelasianum),* ed. L. C. Mohlberg, Herder, Rome, 3rd edition, 1981, *Rerum ecclesiasticarum documenta,* Series major IV, n. 450.

²⁸* "... ipse te linit chrismate salutis, ut eius aggregatus populo Christi sacerdotis, prophetae et regis membra permaneas in vitam aeternam."

²⁹* *Ordo romanus XI,* ed. M. Andrieu, "Les Ordines romains du haut moyen âge," *Spicilegium Sacrum Lovaniense,* Louvain, 1960, vol. 2, Les textes, 416-447.

³⁰* *Le Pontifical romano-germanique du Xième siècle,* eds. C. Vogel-R. Elze, Città del Vaticano, 1963, vol. 2, Studi e testi 227, 108, nn. 381-389.

³¹* *Le Pontifical romain au moyen âge.* Ed. M. Andrieu, vol. 1, *Le Pontifical romain du XIIième siècle.* Città del Vaticano, 1938, Studi e Testi 86, XXXII, 35, 247-248.

³²* *Le Pontifical romain au XIIIième siècle.* Ed. M. Andrieu, Città del Vaticano, 1940, XXIV, 2-3, 452.

³³* *Le Pontifical romain au moyen âge.* Ed. M. Andrieu, vol. 3, *Le Pontifical de Guillaume Durand,* Lib. I, 1-18, 333-335.

³⁴* *"Qua propter,* ut ritus confirmationis *ad ipsam etiam ritus sacramentalis esentiam congruenter pertineat,* Suprema Nostra Auctoritate Apostolica *decernimus et consitutuimus,* ut ea que sequuntur, in *Ecclesia latina in posterum servantur:* SACRAMENTUM CONFIRMATIONIS CONFERTUR *"PER UNCTIONEM CHRISTMATIS IN FRONTE,"* QUAE FIT *"MANUS IMPOSITIONE"* ATQUE PER VERBA *"ACCIPE SIGNACULUM DONI SPIRITUS SANCTI."*

³⁵* On this subject, see L. Ligier, *La confirmation,* Paris, Beauchesne 1973, Théologie historique 23, 28ff.

³⁶* Hippolytus of Rome, *La Tradition Apostolique,* ed. B. Botte, Münster W. LQF 39, c. 21, 52-53.

³⁷* *Liber sacramentorum romanae Aeclesiae ordinis anni circuli.* Ed. L. C. Mohlberg. *Rerum Ecclesiasticarum Documenta,* Fontes IV, Rome, Herder 1981, 3rd ed., 74, nn. 450-451.

³⁸* *Liber sacramentorum Gellonensis,* ed. A. Dumas, Turnhout, 1981, CCL CLIX, 100, n. 710.

³⁹* *Le Pontifical romano-germanique du Xième siècle,* eds. C. Vogel-R. Elze, vol. 2 Texte, Studi e Testi 227, Città del Vaticano, 1963, 109.

⁴⁰* *Le Pontifical romain au XIIième siècle,* ed. M. Andrieu, *Le Pontifical romain au moyen âge,* vol. 1, Studi e Testi 86, Città del Vaticano, 1938, 247.

⁴¹* *Le Pontifical de la Curie romaine au XIIIième siècle,* ed. M. Andrieu, *Le Pontifical romain au moyen âge,* vol. 2, Studi e Testi 87, Città del Vaticano, 1940, 452.

⁴²* *Le Pontifical de Guillaume Durand,* ed. M. Andrieu, *Le Pontifical romain au moyen âge,* vol. 3, Studi e Testi 88, Città del Vaticano, 1940, 333.

⁴³* *Sacrosanctum Concilium,* n. 21.

⁴⁴* See p. 105. We address again synthetically the problem of the anointing: The prayer which accompanies the postbaptismal anointing goes back to the *De sacramentis* of St. Ambrose (II, 24; ed. B. Botte, Sources Chré-

tiennes 25 bis, 88). It was reproduced almost word for word by the *Gelasian Sacramentary* (ed. Mohlberg, n. 450). Our present *Ordo* for baptism has added a new ending to this prayer, intended to emphasize the gift of priesthood to the baptized: *ut eius populo Christi sacerdotis prophetae et regis membrum permaneas in vitam aeternam.*" However, Hugues of St. Victor, who saw that the separation between baptism and confirmation led to the neglect of the latter, wrote in order to insist upon the importance of confirmation: "Propterea ex quo nomine (christianitatis) omnes communicantes coeperunt, omnes unctionem accipere debuerunt, quia in Christo omnes genus electum sumus et regale sacerdotium." (*Dogmatica*, pars VII, *De confirmatione*, *PL* 176, 459—A. Nocent, "L'Ordo lectionum et la confirmation," in *Mens concordet voci*, *Mélanges Martimort*, Paris, 1983, 592.

⁴⁵* "Sacramentum confirmationis confertur per manus vel manuum impositionem et unctionem in fronte cum verbis: Accipe signaculum doni Spiritus Sancti."

⁴⁶* "Episcopus solus manum (vel manus) imponit super confirmandos. Si confirmandi non sunt numerosi, Episcopus manum super singulos imponere potest duplici modo: seu dicendo orationem 'Deus omnipotens' per singulos, seu dicendo hanc orationem super omnes imponendo manum, postea imponendo manum super singlos nihil dicens."

"Si confimandi sunt numerosi, episcopus dicit orationem imponendo manus super omnes simul."

"Universus ritus duplicem significationem praebet. Per impositionem manus vel manuum super confirmandos ab episcopo factam, biblicus gestus exprimitur quo Spiritus Sanctus invocatur, modo optime aptato intelligentiae populi christiani. Ut veritas textus verificetur, ad invocationem Episcopo manum imponentis Spiritus Sanctur infunditur. In unctione chrismatis atque in verbis quae illam comitantur, clare effectus doni Spiritus Sancti significatur. Oleo odorato. . . ."

⁴⁷* "Deinde episcopus solus manum vel manus super omnes confirmandos imponit, dicens:. . . ."

⁴⁸* "Episcopus, si confirmandi non sunt numerosi vel sibi opportunum videtur, duplici modo confirmare potest: Stans, extendit manus super omnes confirmandos dicendo. . . . Deinde Episcopus sedet et imponit manum super caput singulorum, nihil dicens. Vel: Epicopus sedet et imponit manum super singulos dicendo ad singulos orationem Deus omnipotens. . . ."

3 The Sacrament of Reconciliation

On December 2, 1973 the *Ordo of Penance* was promulgated. It was not received with much enthusiasm, it must be said: A number of persons were expecting much more from it—doubtless too much—or else they expected some subjective solutions not in harmony with the authenticity of a true conversion. Before we reexamine the *Ordo,* and in order to be sure we remain objective throughout, we must recall that what is fundamental is not the absolution, but the conversion. NO ritual can dispense from this conversion: On the contrary, ritual must lead to conversion and be its culmination. Keeping this fundamental notion in mind, we can proceed to a critical reading of the new ritual and make a few suggestions for change.

First, there are two rather astonishing points for comment in this *Ordo.* The first is the title: *Ordo paenitentiae.* For in fact the introduction to the rituals employs consistently the term "reconciliation," a new and very rich terminology. It occurs more than twenty times in the introduction, and the decree of promulgation also uses the expression. We welcome this new terminology, for it avoids the somewhat juridical character sometimes associated with this sacrament. St. Paul uses the term, which for him means the relationship between God and us, and he stresses that it is God who takes the initiative to effect this reconciliation (Rom 5:10-11; 11:15; 2 Cor 5:17-21; Col 1:19-25; Eph 2:14-17). The introduction begins with a presentation of the mystery of reconciliation, and it emphasizes the victorious initiative of the Father, who has reconciled the world to himself through Christ, by reestablishing peace. It is therefore astonishing that the *Ordo* did not use the term "reconciliation" in its title, a word that possesses much richer meaning. We find precedent in tradition, moreover, for this term: In fact, the *Gelasian Sacramentary* has the title *Item ad reconciliandum paenitentem*[1]*; the *Pontifical of the Roman Curia of the thirteenth century* has *Ordo ad reconciliandum paenitentem.*[2]*

A second remark: It seems a shame that the new *Ordo* presents us first with the ritual intended for a single penitent. Both the introduction and the official decrees themselves are clear about the special value that they accord to the communal aspect of the sacrament. Since this is so, why not have given first place to the ritual for the reconciliation of several penitents, as the preferred example? The *Ordo reconciliationis* would therefore have been structured as follows: (1) Ordo of reconciliation for several penitents, with individual confession; (2) Ordo of reconcilation for a single penitent; (3) Ordo of reconciliation for several pentitents, with general absolution without previous individual confession.

It will be noted that not only does this schema change the order of the headings—for reasons explained above—but also their wording. An explanation will follow below.

First however, let us take a look at the order of the headings, along with the headings found in the ritual of 1973.

1. The Ritual for a Single Penitent

In the abstract, it is an excellent ritual if the penitents are not numerous. For instance, if there are more than two penitents at the same time, a fourth would have to wait around forty minutes for it to be his or her turn. If there are a certain number of confessions, it becomes impractical. In fact, if there are more than ten or so penitents the priest will have trouble using the entire prayer, and must limit himself to the absolution strictly speaking— that is to say, the end of the prayer "I absolve you of all your sins." We must be honest enough to admit that at this point we are back to earlier usage.

Still, it is a ritual that should be kept and commended, where it is possible to use it as it is: For an individual confession in the rectory, for instance, or in a religious community during a spiritual exercise, where the penitents can wait.

This brings us to the reflection that it might be good to have a ritual for several penitents besides the one we have now, similar but more easily "handled." When the confessor sees that more than two or three penitents are waiting for him, he could, in a simple ceremony, make the ritual for a single penitent into a collective celebration: First, a welcoming address to the little group, a brief reading from Scripture, and the examination of conscience. Next, each penitent makes confession and receives the penance that he or she must make, and then absolution. (We will return to this subject of this individual absolution after the confession of each penitent.) The celebration ends with a short act of thanksgiving, said by all at the same time. In other words, this is the second ritual for several penitents in a somewhat reduced form.

However, another remark must be made concerning all the rituals and the prayer of absolution itself. This prayer even as it is represents considerable progress over the preceeding ritual of Paul V, which was almost exclusively juridical: "I absolve you of all you sins. . . ." It is not, however, without its weak points. Even while it expresses correctly the paschal aspect of reconciliation, the intervention of the Spirit and the ministry of the Church, it nevertheless does not emphasize the fact that reconciliation concerns not only God, but the Church as well, with whom the penitent must be reconciled. Not only is the penitent helped by the ministry of the Church, but he or she must also be reconciled with the Church.

The prayer, moreover, labors under a burdensome linguistic flaw. It starts out in the third person: "Father of mercy, who. . . ." and ends in the first person: "I absolve you. . . ." In other words, it is not clear who is doing the absolving. From the point of view of linguistics, this is not an acceptable formulation, and it is to be regretted that such a recent ritual was accepted despite such a serious flaw.

But there is more, and this time we are faced with the sort of theology that we encountered in our discussion of the prayer of baptism using the triple interrogation. Until the end of the thirteenth century, the Latin Church used a deprecatory prayer, as is still done in the Eastern liturgies. This deprecatory prayer along with the imposition of the hands is sufficient to express the authoritative intercession. But it would seem that it was not felt to be enough, whence the addition of the juridical formula: "And

I absolve you. . . ." And adding further to the emphasis laid on this ending phrase, it is printed in bold type. This could not help but lead to what has become general practice. This is often the only sentence said by the priest. It cannot be denied that in many countries and parishes the ritual used is, once again, that of the days before Vatican II—the simple juridical formulation: "I absolve you. . . ." On the other hand, we cannot expect the prayer to somehow square the circle: In order for it to say what it must say, it could hardly be shorter.

One last remark seems called for: In the case of the confession of a single penitent, why is there only one form of absolution available to the priest? The fact that only one formulation has been provided has eliminated the possibility of expressing one very important dimension of the sacrament, and that is its relationship with the Eucharist. For there is only one prayer for both venial and mortal sins. All that would have been needed was an ending phrase that, in the case of serious sin, added the words "which grants you forgiveness and peace, and restores you to the table of his Eucharist." Different words could have been used, as, for instance, for children, etc. Since we have a choice of Eucharistic prayers, why not have several different forms of absolution?

2. Rituals for Several Penitents with Individual Confession

We should note that this heading does not reproduce what was given officially by the *Ordo paenitentiae,* which adds, in fact, *"and with individual absolution."* It should be noted also that the heading of this paragraph is in the plural: *Rituals.* In fact, if the absolution could be collective after individual confession, several forms of rituals could be imagined, as we shall try to show.

The majority of documents consider individual confession to be absolutely necessary. On June 19, 1972, the Congregation for the Doctrine of the Faith reiterated the absolute obligation, except in emergencies, of a complete individual confession of serious sins.[3*] On November 13, 1972, the Canadian bishops Conference insisted on individual confession and stressed its importance: It ensures the stability of the sinner's conversion, it makes clear the steps which the Lord wants the penitent to take in order to leave behind his or her path of error. It also shows how the penitent may make amends for any harm he or she has done, and may remove any scandal his or her behavior may have given. All of this reflects a personal welcoming of reconciliation within the Church community. In other words, the Canadian Commission puts great emphasis on the element of "conversion" which is so essential and important in the case of a sinner.[4]*

The doctrinal commission of the Belgium episcopate often demands individual confession, even after general absolution. The text explains why the Church continues to demand the individual owning of serious sins. Such sins, says the document, causes a serious rift within the personality and with his or her relationship with Christ and the Church. For this reason a sort of journey is demanded of the penitent, a journey of conversion definitely personalized, and expressed and lived within the Church.[5]* A document like this is therefore deeply attentive to the conversion of the sinner, and rightly so. Absolution, even if it brings with it the grace of healing, does not act magically. Care must be taken that the sinner make personal efforts towards conversion, and all possible ways to help him or her progress towards conversion must be implemented.

But let us leave aside the obligation of individual confession; in the present climate of the Western Church and her members it seems that it cannot be dispensed with. Note that we have written: ". . . in the present climate of the Western Church and her members." What precisely does this phrase mean? If indeed individual confession is intended to guarantee personal conversion and perseverance, could there not be a substitute for it, not in order to avoid a painful avowal of sin, but in order to lead more surely to personal conversion? Let us give an example: During the season of Eastertide confessions, it often happens that the priest hearing confessions hears important confidences. He would like to attempt some healing of the penitent, but this would mean conversation of some length, which is impossible because of the numbers of people waiting. Just how efficacious is this contact with the priest in confession, under such circmstances? Is it absolutely necessary that absolution be given immediately, at the time of the avowal of sin. Could it not be sometimes more efficacious for the penitent, after making confession, to be invited first to accomplish some penance with the obligation of seeing the confessor at a later time, without receiving absolution until satisfaction for the sin is made?

What we are talking about here is really a return to the ancient discipline of penance, but without the same obligation, with the confessor free to use his judgment depending upon the circumstances. Such a procedure was for a long time the practice of the Church, even after canonical public confession was abandoned.[6]*

When individual confession is practiced, except in emergencies, the question of immediate absolution then arises, as we have seen above. But there is yet another question. It is astonishing that the collective absolution *of those who have already confessed* is rarely, or even never, addressed. This is an entirely different case from that of collective absolution without previous confession. In this last case, personal conversion is not particularly ensured—what is stressed is the absolution. But in the suggestion we make here, the avowal of sins has taken place.

Why would the collective absolution of those who have already made confession be desirable? The obvious answer is: To emphasize the communal aspect of the sin and its absolution. Is there any theological objection to doing this? I do not think so. Such was the practice of the Church for centuries, for public penitence. The penitents made their confession to the priest, and once they had made satisfaction they were presented to the bishop, who gave them all absolution. There is no real reason why the same person must hear the confession and also give the absolution, for once the penitent has made confession and the priest has heard the case, the priest can then give permission for receiving absolution. In any case, this was indeed Church practice.[7]*

Does this way of proceeding present any advantages? We have just emphasized one: Collective absolution brings out the social aspect of sin and reconciliation. Moreover, this suggestion opens the door to a number of excellent possibilities. Let us note a few of them. The confessor who is called by several penitents, four or five, or even fewer, says a word of welcome to them. He reads to them a brief passage from Scripture, allows some time for individual examination of conscience (or leads one), hears confessions, and then gives absolution to those who have confessed and can thus receive absolution. In a religious community, the confessor arrives in the morning, and the first part of the ritual of reconciliation is celebrated, up to the examination of conscience. Those religious who so desire make their confession during the day when they have time, and in the evening those who have confessed receive absolution, and all celebrate an act of thanksgiving. In a parish community, a day is set for confessions; the first part of the celebration takes place up to the examination of conscience, and then one or two days are taken up in hearing confessions. On a specified later day, those who have confessed receive absolution, and together all celebrate an act of thanksgiving.

Are there then any reasons not to do things this way? To do this presupposes a serious catechesis and also some form of preaching before absolution is given. The person who is about to absolve should say: "The absolution which is about to be given is only valid for those who have had their confessions heard and who have then received permission to receive absolution from their confessor." This would be at the same time a good catechesis of the efficacity of the sacrament: The absolution has no value unless the penitent has made confession and if the confessor judges that he or she can receive the absolution. So it is clear that absolution in itself has no mechanical effect. Lastly, we must clearly distinguish this collective absolution after individual confession from collective absolution given without prior confession.

However, we must observe fully the present discipline which is the will of the Church. Such collective absolution, even given after confession, is not permitted without the authorization of the bishop.

I do not think that there is any need to worry that misunderstandings will lead, for instance, to some who have not made confession thinking that they can benefit from collective absolution: A very clear short sermon before the absolution ought to suffice to avoid any such confusion. In a number of monasteries there was the custom to give to the entire community, four times a year during major feasts, a general absolution. There was a very specific ritual for this practice. Since Vatican II, most monasteries have eliminated this practice. But it is clear that no monk or nun thought that such a general absolution carried with it absolution for serious sin.

Yet there is another disciplinary practice that must be scrupulously respected, even while it is not easy to understand, and that is the practice of never, under any circumstances, joining the sacrament of reconciliation with the celebration of the Eucharist. It is quite clear that this is forbidden, but nowhere can we find a precise explanation why. And it is true that there are not many examples from the past of linking the two sacraments. Among the ancient texts brought together by Dom Edmond Martène there is only one, from the eleventh century, in Evreux.[8]*

This rule seems strange. For in fact the words of the consecration remind us that Christ's blood was shed for the remission of sins. All the sacraments are, or can be, inserted into the Liturgy of the Word and the Eucharist, except the sacrament of the remission of sins, which the Eucharistic celebration expressly stresses in its central text.

How are we to understand this rule? It becomes immediately understandable if we are talking about inserting confessions and absolutions into the Eucharistic celebration. But it is no longer so easy to understand if absolution alone is given to those who have made confession outside of Mass.

It is well known that some feel that neither confession nor absolution are necessary at all, since the Eucharist remits sins. It is not our purpose here to discuss this claim, but it is still of use to point out that each sacrament has its own individual efficacity. Undoubtedly, every sacrament is in some way dependent upon the Eucharist, in that the Eucharist actualizes the sacrifice of Christ, from which all grace flows. Every sacrament also leads up to the Eucharist. And this is true also of the sacrament of reconciliation: It derives its efficacity from the sacrifice of Christ and it leads to the Eucharist, but it is specifically the sacrament which, deriving from the sacrifice of Christ, forgives those sins committed since baptism. It would seem that, if the sacrament of reconciliation were celebrated during the Eucharistic celebration, the union of the two sacraments would be clearly brought to the fore, as well as the specificity of the sacrament of penitence through which the baptized must pass in order to obtain the remission of his or her present sins.

This rule forbidding such a practice can be understood if the suggestion were made to insert confessions into the Mass, but, however that may be, the rule stands and must be observed. It may be permitted, however, to regret that such severity is absent when it comes to the practice of hearing confessions during Mass. Clearly these confessions are not linked to the Eucharist—but they are parallel. Two celebrations are going on, not at the same time, since the sacrament of penitence is not linked to the Eucharist, but they are juxtaposed. It would admittedly be something new altogether to intercalate the sacrament of penitence into the celebration of the Eucharist, but still, are we not destroying both by making them parallel to each other?

3. The Ritual for Collective Absolution Without Prior Individual Confession

There is no need here to repeat the conditions necessary for this ritual. It is obvious that, by itself, it does not encourage personal conversion, but rather centers on absolution. It is easy to understand why the Church does not encourage it. There are, however, cases where such a ritual may be necessary. We shall not go into these questions of application here. From the point of view of the ritual, our remarks on the other rituals are sufficient. The one point to make might be that the short sermon before the ritual should make plain the conditions for the absolution to be legitimate; it should mention the authorization of the bishop, and it should remind the penitents of what remains to be done after absolution, etc.

At this point we might present the following synthesis of two main groups of remarks concerning what it might be desirable to effect for the celebration of the sacrament of reconciliation:

Clarify certain rules forbidding some practices, or at least reexamine them—for instance, collective absolution for those who have made confession, and the possibility of inserting collective absolution of those who have confessed after the Gospel of the Mass.

Find an acceptable linguistic framework for our present formula of absolution. Certain specific formulations could be created for particular cases, as, for instance, serious sins, children, etc. If it should be possible to put off absolution, a new prayer of blessing or one of imposing the penance needs to be created. The *Gelasian Sacramentary* gives us good examples,[9]* but various other solutions are possible and could be considered.

Notes

¹* See 360; or also *Reconciliatio paenitentis ad mortem,* 364.

²* M. Andrieu, *Le Pontifical romain au moyen âge,* Vol. II *Le Pontifical de la Curie romaine au XIIIe siècle,* Vatican City 1940, Studi e Testi 87, 484.

³* *Acta Apostolicae Sedis* 64, 1972, 51-514.

⁴* Canadian Episcopate, *La réconciliation,* "Documentation catholique", 57, 1975, 484-486. See also: Msrg. Gréggoire, Bishop of Montreal, *Directives pour les célébrations pénitentielles à l'occasion de Noel* (Dec. 7, 1972). "Documentation catholique" 55, 1973, 292-293.

⁵* Doctrinal Commission of the Conference of Belgian Bishops. *Orientations pour le renouveau de la pratique pénitentielle* (December 1973), "Documentation catholique" 54, 1972, 1122-1125.

⁶* A number of examples can be found in the rituals transcribed by E. Martène. These *Ordines* present considerable interest for us today, even for pastoral reasons. A. Nocent, *La Pénitence dans les Ordines locaux transcrits dans le De Antiquis ecclesiae Ritibus d'Edmond Martène, Paschale Mysterium,* Studia Anselmiana, 91, Analecta Liturgica 10, 1986, 115-138.

⁷* See, for example, M. Andrieu, *Le Pontifical romain au moyen âge,* Vol. III. *Le Pontifical de Guillaume Durand,* Vatican City, 1940, Studi e Testi 88, 560. The priests hear confession; then there is a meeting with the bishop before he gives absolution, in order to find out who is worthy of being absolved. What we have here is an absolution given by the bishop, but it is the priests who have heard the confessions. So it was not considered necessary to have the same priest give absolution as heard the confession. However, the priest who heard the confession makes the decision as to whether a given penitent is worthy of receiving absolution, given here, by the bishop.

⁸* The Ordo of Evreux, eleventh century. See A.-G. Martimort, *La documentation liturgique de dom Edmond Martène,* Vatican City, 1878, Studi e Testi 279, 607; 114; Cf. A. Nocent, *Art. cit.,* 129.

⁹* See *Orationes super paenitentes,* nn. 78-82.

4 An Overview

1. The Essential Reasons for Renewal

In this concluding chapter we should like to go beyond the particular issues which we looked at in the preceding chapters and address the question of what constitutes the essence of the impact that we can attribute to the renewal of the liturgy. We do not mean some sort of evaluation of its success or lack of it, but rather an overview of whether or not the pre-conciliary study, the decisions of the Council, and their application have carried out the purpose of the Church.

Liturgical renewal did not take place in response to any passing caprice nor any poorly-defined desire for change for change's sake. The Constitution on the Liturgy expressed very clearly the goals of the renewal that it called for, goals that constituted a vital rediscovery of the very nature of liturgy itself. At numbers 5 through 11 it explains succinctly and clearly what the term liturgy means. Through the liturgy we become contemporaries of events of salvation that happened in the past, and we become authors of the reconstruction of the world, living the past in acts and turned toward the future. The Constitution declares for our benefit that the liturgy is the high point of the activity of the Church, which has no more important role to fulfill.

So the liturgy is not to be reduced to the level of any other means of communication: It is THE means of communication par excellence—through it we become what it communicates, as it sweeps us up in its activity. In and through the liturgy we become a priestly people. The liturgy gives us the power to act in concert with itself.

This is the whole purpose of liturgical renewal, and the renewal sanctioned by Vatican Council II consists in making available to all, whatever may be his or her level of education, the contents of the liturgy in all its various forms. The documents relative to the application of renewal therefore deal with the how and why of renewal: What is already in place should not be altered unless there is real necessity; in order to make a particular change, an historical study must take place first so that what is essential and must not be altered is differentiated from what is peripheral. This work of adaptation and sometimes of creation takes place on two levels, without being too rigid about it: The adaptation itself is reserved to central Authority and the bishops, whereas particular accommodation to specific situations is the responsibility of the ministers of each celebration. This represents a lot of work, which is very time-consuming and supposes considerable competence and patient study. It is easy to understand that the responsibility of working with such a rich and delicate tool cannot be entrusted to just anybody. Renewal does not call for change for change's sake, nor does it leave any room for personal caprice to make changes that please just one individual or even a particular group of individuals. Adaptation must work from the particular outwards towards the universal, which is the hallmark of the Church.

2. A Paradoxical Situation

It is an unfortunate fact that the material whose theoretical basis we have studied has not been the subject of an adequate catechesis, and the greater number of the faithful and even priests have used the changes of this adaptation without really understanding the reasons behind them. Many have been scandalized by them and have adopted an attitude of defiance, more or less entrenched. There are other ways of handling the situation and it takes no time at all to make pertinent suggestions: It is another matter altogether to change mentalities, a goal which can take fifty or even a hundred years of patient effort.

3. The Crisis of the Sacred

Yet there is more. The renewal of the liturgy took place just as we were experiencing the phenomenon of the secularization of society. If the latter must be rejected because it is destructive of the most basic elements of faith, which is contravened, it must be said, by the desire to bring everything under the control of reason alone, nevertheless we have no reason to condemn out of hand a balanced degree of secularization which in fact may bring out the special nature of the sacred, by reducing a surfeit of sacralization which ends up weakening the sense of the sacred by smothering it. The renewal of the liturgy has nothing to fear from secularization—on the contrary, to the degree to which it brings out the contrast between what is essential and what is superfluous overgrowth, it can actually help the cause of renewal. What is truly sacred, what is essential, will stand forth clearly again. Of course, distinguishing carefully between the two is a delicate operation not without its dangers, and regrettable excesses are possible.

And this has been, unfortunately, the case only too frequently. This was to some extent the result of a previous state of "rubricism" in the liturgy that we were just beginning to get away from—a situation so stifling that many still defined the liturgy as a collection of rubrics ruling what goes on in every ceremony, like some courtly etiquette. Even recently, in one of the major theological seminaries, some thirty future priests could not give a definition of the liturgy and ended up reducing it to a code of laws.

On the other hand, another group overly appreciative of secularization went overboard with childish enthusiasm and destructively wanted to get rid of everything they judged superfluous and not truly in the domain of the sacred. There is not one of us who cannot give an example of these numerous excesses, this total lack of sound judgment. For instance, the altar is only a table that is needed temporarily for the Eucharistic celebration; the meaning of the Eucharistic celebration is best expressed when is takes place like an ordinary meal; clothing worn should be everyday and no special vestments should be worn by the celebrants; a priest in everyday clothing who happens to be in the congregation should not hesitate to raise his hands in unity with what is going on at the altar; no chalice is needed, a regular glass is fine; a stole put on over a sweater is all that is needed for celebrating Mass, which can take place with everyone sitting on the floor around a coffee table full of sandwiches and glasses of wine— and more such scandalous stuff which should not be laid at the door of mere negligence, but rather of a conscious desire for adaptation which pretends to be following the bent of renewal out of what is seen as pastoral concern. All this can almost lead one to sympathize with the attitudes of the most rigid traditionalists, without going to their excessively reactionary lengths. Fortunately such practices as we have enumerated do seem to be less and less frequent these days.

4. The Impact of Intellectualism

Leaving behind these cruder misapplications of liturgical renewal, let us take a look at yet another attitude, a paradoxical one this time, that is much subtler and will show up in the attempts at renewal imposed by the Church at Vatican II.

The work of liturgical renewal had to beware of a tendency that it was only too easy for the specialists in the history of the liturgy to give in to. The method imposed by Vatican II called for a profound historical study of each celebration that was going to be subject to the work of renewal with a view to making it more accessible. The Constitution on the Liturgy did not hesitate to acknowledge that, over the centuries, liturgical celebrations sometimes became burdened by a whole series of peripheral practices which, in many cases, made understanding more difficult. The Constitution called for rituals that could be easily grasped without giving long explanations. An historical study of a liturgical celebration ought to make obvious what is essential to the ritual and what are the superfluous additions. This is easy to say, but it is another matter to carry out such a directive with objectivity and prudence.

One example of a sharp reaction to the introduction of such a peripheral practice during the Easter Vigil will make this clear: The famous letter of St. Jerome on the blessing and use of the paschal candle, which had become the practice in communities even up to the gates of Rome itself. The rapier-like pen of St. Jerome, whose character as we well know was quite emotional and given to subjective judgments, denounced this new symbolic practice of the lighting and the blessing of the paschal candle as a "vanity" which was trying to infiltrate the sober liturgy of Rome. Jerome was not able to appreciate the symbolism which had seduced the Churches of his time and he did not hesitate to condemn its practice at Rome; in fact, this practice did not figure in papal liturgy until quite late, undoubtedly due to the influence of St. Jerome.

Studying the history of the liturgy for the sake of renewal could have led to some regrettable archaisms, and voices were raised to that effect. But such study could just as well lead to the restoration of certain practices that had begun by answering a purely practical need, such as the paschal candle, necessary for giving light during a nighttime celebration, and which afterwards became a symbol of Christ as the Light of the World. Many other examples could be adduced here: In the earliest times, when the Christians gathered together to celebrate had to act in secrecy, the altar was only an indispensable table. In fact, the early Christians stated with pride that they did not have an altar—they themselves were the altar. This is of course true, but it does not necessarily mean that we must refuse to accept the symbolism of the altar as Christ, a symbolism that appeared quite early. Another example: Adding water to the wine was necessary in antiquity when wine was a concentrated, almost syrupy drink that everyone diluted before drinking. But very early on this practice acquired the symbolism of the mixture, in Christ, of divinity and humanity, or yet again, of the water that flowed from the side of Christ. Obviously, none of this symbolism is necessary for the celebration of the Eucharist, but for that reason should we eliminate all of it?

The allegation has sometimes been made that liturgical renewal was "too French," that is, intellectualist, even Cartesian. Without totally agreeing, we might have to admit that a certain tendency in this direction has not always been absent from the work of renewal, which has sometimes been quite severe in getting rid of symbolic practices. But we see such dry, rationalistic attitudes even more in the application of the recommendations of renewal than in the texts themselves. This was true twenty-five years ago and is still true today. For example, the texts of renewal did not call for total suppression of the use of incense, even if it allows great latitude in such use. Equally, the use of candles and other lights was not limited to the one traditional candle, or even prohibited altogether. Liturgical vestments were not eliminated, neither for solemn offices nor above all for the celebration of the Eucharist, for which the priest who officiates alone, or who leads a concelebration, must always wear the chasuble, despite frequent practice to the contrary in our day. Again, statues of the saints have not been prohibited, even though some judgment as to their relative symbolic value was called for—a statue of a minor saint should not be twice as big as one of Christ, nor placed in a more imposing and visible location; nor should such statuary be overwhelming in the overall esthetic of the building. Renewal did not call for the suppression of all processions, neither for the entrance of the Eucharistic celebration nor for Divine Office, or the procession before the Gospel reading. We could continue this enumeration of the practices that a certain number would have liked to see eliminated for the sake of a return to essential roots, not without being tinged with some degree of secularism, it must be said.

Liturgical renewal has had its run of bad luck. On the one hand, it comes up against a very strong degree of secularization in society as a whole, and yet, on the other hand, in that same society there is an ever greater demand for what could be called the "audio-visual," and even more the "visual" than the "audio." This is a situation to which we must pay some attention.

5. An Impossible Balance?

No matter how we may feel about it, it is an eluctable fact that our society today needs to touch and feel. There is no reason to be unduly alarmed about this, either—knowledge, for the ancient Semites, those of the Bible, is based on hearing, seeing, and touching. When St. John tells us that he has known the Word of God, by "known" he means that he saw him and touched him. In our Roman liturgy, in one of the Prefaces of Christmas, it is said that from now on we know God by seeing him. Christianity is a religion of incarnation and not of abstraction. Even the most abstract theory of knowledge will tell us that we know nothing intellectually that has not first entered into our minds through our senses.

But what should alarm us in the culture of today is the tendency of the "package" to assume more importance than its contents—taking so much more pleasure in what is seen than what the attractive "package" contains is relegated to second place, whether we are talking about visual or auditory packaging. This was a danger already seen by St. Paul who spoke of certain groups who at times gave more attention to the pleasure of listening to fine speeches and interesting stories than to the meaning they contained. He was quite right, and what he enveighed against so long ago is all too often the case today.

This is all basically a question of imbalance. It is a problem that can be solved. Liturgical renewal cannot ignore this "audiovisual" thrust of modern society, and in fact we cannot say that it has—in general, it has left the field open for visual effect, for the presence of the symbolic, and for auditory appeal. But these are applications which have not always been followed and which sometimes go to two different and unfortunate extremes: Either an excessive over-simplification of the rituals and a distaste for all symbolism, or, on the other hand, an overabundance of visual effects that end up masking the contents of a particular celebration and the meaning that it should express. There is often in these cases a desire for creativity that is mostly poorly inspired and awkwardly applied.

We must of course give concrete examples, but in so doing try to avoid what might be seen as an attitude of condemnation, a sort of bitterness which has often cast discredit on liturgical renewal which is then considered, without making any distinctions, the root of all the excesses, and therefore rejected without further thought.

The first attitude, then, wants a return to the essential, ignoring all evolution, and calls for a total denuding of the liturgy of all non-essentials, as if this were the sole way for the liturgy to hand down the means of salvation. This is a sort of false interpretation of "worship in spirit and in truth."

Not everything in this attitude is to be rejected. All one has to do is open the liturgical books and, beginning with the oldest, see all the successive enrichments which corresonded to a certain mentality and a certain point in time. Not all were truly enriching, and they ended up only too often by obscuring what ought to have been given the limelight. There are plenty of examples; let us cite just a few.

Taking a look at the first pontificals, which contain those celebrations reserved to the bishop, we see from century to century how the number and diversity of benedictions were increased. We ended up by blessing everything, and so everything became more or less sacred. It is easy to see that such an overabundance could lead to severe eliminations, even though these must be done carefully.

The ordinations of bishops, priests, and deacons are well-known examples. Their basis is the imposition of hands with a prayer. From century to century we see a whole series of elements introduced: Anointings, the handing over of instruments, the evangeliary, a chalice, etc. By the time of Pope Pius XII, the Holy Father had to ponder the question of what the rituals were which actually confer holy orders. A careful study of the documents permitted the conclusion that the imposition of hands alone is the essential ritual conferring orders in a valid way. But this did not mean that the other complementary rituals were suppressed.

It can happen that certain rituals which were appropriate for a given time have become for us purely ceremonial and hide the real meaning of what is being celebrated. There has been so much exteriorization that the authenticity even of some vestments and some ways of standing, sitting, etc., during the ceremony has become open to question. Even today it can happen that the desire for a particular ceremonial act can lead to the neglect of something authentic and essential. When a priest puts on the vestments of a deacon, when an archbishop receives the title of deacon, when a layperson proclaims the Gospel, we have ceremonial situations which are not authentic. And a celebration can be overwhelming in majesty and pomp, but disappointing in the poverty or inappropriateness of its contents. This is pure ceremony, void of authenticity.

These situations, all too frequent, arise from a certain iconoclastic desire to eliminate everything that is not essential to a given celebration. Of course, it is not the fact that the cantor wears a cope that is important, but that he should sing his verses with dignity, and well. But even when it is based on some justifiable attitudes, no iconoclasticism bears good fruit. In our case, giving up every gesture that is not strictly necessary, and every bit of symbolism, in order to feel secure that one has found the real and the authentic is not the best solution.

Then there is the other camp, where the "audio-visual" takes priority, to the detriment of the contents. We must sing, as much as possible, and of course in the language of the people. It does not matter that the music is mediocre, that the words do not match the meaning of what is being celebrated. What is most important is that the assembly be brought out of themselves, stimulated, in a sort of collective state of excitement which goes by the name of participation. This is certainly excessive, but does not mean that a sane use of the audio-visual cannot be of use, especially as the texts already recommend in their somewhat secularized rules.

But if we are searching for visual effects, why should we reject what the Church itself already offers? Let us give a few examples. One of the more striking ones is the Gospel procession. If there is a well-balanced and appropriate "video" effect for today, it is certainly this procession. What better way to express the authenticity of the book and the respect that is its due? In several countries a special evangeliary is published which facilitates this act of showing particular respect during a celebration for the words of Christ and the Gospel which contains them. It seems only reasonable that this book be an appropriately well-bound copy. If it is carried in procession at the beginning of the celebration of the Eucharist and placed respectfully on the altar, this provides an excellent catechesis by itself. If the evangeliary is proclaimed with lights and incense and presented open towards the assembly, the symbolism of Christ himself present in his words and turned towards his people is not lost on anyone. Such symbolic acts are truly authentic and are particularly well-adapted to the culture of today. Why should we deprive our popular assemblies in particular of the richness of this ritual? It is truly hard to understand the mentality that wishes to suppress this excellent ritual. And if the rubrics permit incensing the evangeliary, why not respect such a gesture which has centuries of tradition behind it and which expresses perfectly the meaning of the act? The person who proclaims the Gospel announces that the Lord is present: "The Lord be with you." He stops for a moment and, in order to make manifest the glory of this presence, incenses the evangeliary before beginning the proclamation of the Gospel. Why should we replace this authentic ritual with some awkward new invention?

For another matter, after the proclamation of the Gospel, why do we not emphasize again the dynamism of the word by asking the assembly to respond, "Let us acclaim the word of God," while the celebrant raises up the evangeliary for the veneration of all? What valid reasons justify suppressing this ritual? Why should we want to reduce the proclamation of the Gospel to the level of the reading of just any book? Strange and paradoxical reasoning which says it wants to "involve" the faithful, and then does just the opposite.

6. A New Rubricism?

It is astonishing, again, to observe at times what one could call a fad for invention both in gestures and in texts. After turning down what the liturgical books themselves propose and which more often than not is appropriate for our "audio-visual" culture, now we see a certain spirit of contradiction which creates new rituals and words which, it claims, involve the celebrating assembly more. Let us give a few telling examples.

A certain number, fortunately not great, of celebrants want to imitate the Last Supper anecdotally and break the bread at the very moment of consecration: "He took the bread, broke it, and gave it to his disciples." Sacrificing to an anecdotal visual effect, the bread is broken with the words, "he broke it." There is no precedent in the history of liturgy for such anecdotism, and for good reason. During the Last Supper what took place was, first, a blessing over the bread, then the breaking of the bread and its distribution. The Jewish ritual of the paschal meal even today contains these elements. Next comes the meal of the paschal lamb, and then the cup of thanksgiving. The Christian ritual suppresses the meal between the blessing over the bread and the blessing over the cup. If we should want today to reproduce the paschal meal anecdotally, we should break the bread and distribute it immediately. Then the same should be done with the wine. Never has any liturgy tried to so reproduce the paschal meal, which would have made the celebration of our Eucharistic meal very difficult. After all, the celebration of the Eucharist does not consist in imitating the Last Supper any more than it reproduces the sacrifice of the Cross.

It is also craziness to change the texts for no good purpose, just to "personalize" them, as if the priest were not celebrating in the name of Christ and the Church, and as if "making them his own" were not primarily a matter of spiritual interiorization. Here is an example of another unfortunate invention. The concelebrants pass the bread or the chalice to each other, saying to each other: "The Body of Christ, the Blood of Christ," in order to make visible the sharing of Communion. There is no sign of such a practice in any of our liturgies. It is understandable that the priest who has consecrated the bread and gives it to the others should say to the person who receives it, "the Body of Christ": This practice just naturally became part of the liturgy. But what meaning can it possibly have for the priests who have themselves just consecrated the bread and the wine to announce to each other that they are the Body and Blood of Christ? Surely there is no need for this dubious practice.

It is hard to understand why certain time-tested visual rituals should be rejected in favor of the creation of new ones which are not only not licit but are only too obviously devoid of any meaning.

In the last analysis, however, the number of examples that we have cited should not lead us to doubt whether much real progress in renewal has indeed been made. But when there is so much questioning on that very point do we not run the danger of seeing the authorities taking drastic measures which could lead to a new rubricism which would be harmful to the living liturgy? This is a real danger, and if it were to happen we could not fairly point our fingers at Authority alone. . . .

7. An Optimistic Vision

Under no circumstances should the reading of this book be an occasion for downplaying the importance of liturgical renewal, or for rejecting it. It is a matter of basic honesty to acknowledge that renewal has done much good. It is not astonishing that it should have some weak points, which are really only the flip side of the coin. And if in its application there have been mistakes, this does not mean that the documents themselves were at fault. Rather than concentrating on the defects, which need to be pointed out only because they lead to more progress, we should be comforted by the undeniable new sources of holiness and spirituality afforded by the renewal. If we have made a number of criticisms, we need to give just as many examples of the good renewal has done, and these last are much more numerous.

To gauge some of this progress, all one has to do is go into any number of churches and hear the faithful singing. It may not be artistically polished, but the congregation is certainly participating. This is particularly noticeable, in our parishes, during funeral Masses. The congregation listens to the readings and responds appropriately with the responsorials. Over and beyond the celebration of the Eucharist, in some parishes they have organized Liturgies of the Word. There are even places where Lauds and Vespers are sung, at least during certain periods. Meetings of priests too have changed in character, and often begin by the singing of Lauds. And other similar examples of progress should all lead us to conclude that there have been many more advances than losses.

The Church is both human and divine: Its members are what they are with both their good points and their faults, their prejudices and their mentalities, their attachment to what they consider to be tradition. It is the same with the liturgy. We have no reasons to be surprised if there are side-trackings and oppositions, and that this situation will last until the return of Christ. Some wish to return to the bare-bones essentials; the unadorned content is all that counts. For others, the overall atmosphere is central, the general ambiance, the eloquent gestures. Both attitudes contain a portion of the truth. It is the splintering off of one position from the other, in absolutist terms, that slows down the vital pulse of the celebration of a Church. No one should be discouraged, but we all owe it to ourselves to examine our own reactions and their coherence.